Hacking With Linux

Networking Basics and Ethical Hacking for Newbies

Travis Booth

Books by Travis Booth

Scan the Code to Learn More

Machine Learning Series

Machine Learning With Python: Hands-On Learning for Beginners

Machine Learning With Python: An In Depth Guide Beyond the Basics

Python Data Analytics Series

Python Data Analytics: The Beginner's Real World Crash Course

Python Data Analytics: A Hands-On Guide Beyond the Basics

Python Data Science Series

Python Data Science: Hands-On Learning for Beginners

Python Data Science: A Hands-On Guide Beyond the Basics

Deep Learning Series

Deep Learning With Python: A Hands-On Guide for Beginners

Deep Learning With Python: A Comprehensive Guide Beyond the Basics

Bonus Offer: Get the Ebook absolutely free when you purchase the paperback via Kindle Matchbook!

Table of Contents

Introduction

Hackers are basically a cult topic at this point, every other TV show includes a hacker of this or that sort. Usually, hackers are portrayed as the nerdy people that, when they touch a computer, become wizards. This portrayal, unfortunately, is quite inaccurate. Hackers may sometimes have extensive hardware knowledge, however, they won't be hacking into government sites by randomly mashing buttons on a keyboard.

The good part of this is, you don't need to learn how to have godly writing speed in order to become a hacker.

The bad part is, being a hacker is nowhere as flashy as it is on the TV screen.

Being an actual hacker is much closer to solving a math problem than what you see on TV. You're looking for a weakness that a digital entity has and for a way to exploit it. With that being said, little can compare to the feeling that performing your first successful hack gives.

In this book, we'll be teaching you how to do that. Obviously, we won't show you a website, tell you its vulnerabilities and let you hack into it, but we will help you out by teaching you how to do that for yourself. It truly isn't quite as difficult as it seems (unless you're aiming to protect/attack a really important site like say, NASA or the Pentagon.)

We'll be looking at hacking from an analytical standpoint, and we'll throw you right in the gist of things. Currently, you're probably reading this book off of a Windows or Mac PC. Unfortunately, those platforms aren't the best at hacking, so rather than simply teaching you the basics on your platform, we'll teach them to you using the platform that most professional hackers use - Linux.

This book is by no means the extensive database of all hacking knowledge. Keep in mind that I too am human, and prone to making errors. As you grow as a hacker, you'll find parts of this book that you disagree with. I am opinionated after all. In these instances, listen to yourself. Hacking is, at its core, a form of self-expression, and much like an aspiring artist learning to draw, you might look up to someone at the beginning, however, by the end of your journey you should have developed your own style.

It's also worth noting what this book will not teach you:

Programming - If I wanted to teach you programming, this book would be a lot thicker than it already is. This is partly due to hacking requiring endless programming languages to be done successfully a lot of the time. Besides that, I also don't know where your interests lie, whether it's working in cybersecurity for a big firm, or being a grey hat hacker doing online challenges for fun. These two require vastly different skillsets, and I wouldn't want to spread this book too thin, and leave you with basically nothing.

Most black hat hacking techniques - This is where the opinionated part comes in, I don't want to teach you how to be a criminal. Instead of this, we'll be looking at black hat hacking techniques only from an analytical standpoint. We won't go into detail about how specific techniques are performing, unless the detail is crucial to stopping them from ever getting off of the ground. If you're looking for a book that will teach you how to maliciously hack into your friend's Facebook account, you're better off looking elsewhere.

The ins and outs of Linux/Mac/Windows - While for quite a few sorts of hacking, you need in-depth knowledge of your, and your target's/employer's operating systems, we'd need to cover all three. Besides, there have been books much thicker than this one written on the topic by people that know far more about it than I do. We'll only be looking at the parts of Linux that interest you as a basic user and an aspiring hacker.

So, with that being said, what will this book teach you?

The basics of how hackers are segmented - you've definitely heard the terms "white," "black," or "grey" hacker, and you might've been confused as to what they meant. Well, be confused no more! We'll be going through all three of these, as well as some of the more prominent examples of hackers in each of these sorts.

Why you should learn to hack - You definitely already have an interest in hacking, after all, you bought this book. With that being said, I'll be aiming at showing you what motivated many people to actually follow through with it, and become hackers professionally. I'll also be going into some of the more mundane benefits of being a hacker you might not have thought of.

Basic Linux scripting - Scripts are vital to hacking, they're less the main part of the operation (as might seem from pop-culture) and more along the lines of the backbone. They make your job easier, and will teach you to think properly. Naturally, I won't be able to show you every Linux script in existence, nor will you be at an advanced level at the end of this book. With that being said, you'll be good enough to start hacking, and start learning more from other books, as well as your peers and professors.

Cybersecurity - How the field of cybersecurity works, what it does, as well as which main kinds of professions exist for those that learn to be very good at it. We'll be looking at some of the main things that a cybersecurity expert should know how to do in order to be good at their job.

Careers - We'll be checking out how to make a career for yourself as a hacker, as well as the most common positions for hacking experts. It's worth noting that we won't only be looking at positions that are explicitly hacking-related but will also be checking out those that can be done with the knowledge hacking incidentally brings. E.g. If you are a proficient hacker, doing the job of a system administrator would be extremely easy for you.

Now that we've gone through that, let's dive right into the world of hacking.

Chapter 1: So, You Want to Be A Hacker?

In this chapter, we'll be looking at the most common misconceptions about hackers, the kinds of hackers there are, as well as some of the things you'll need in order to become a hacker.

Let's get the first thing out of the way- dedication and passion. Both of these are crucial parts of becoming a successful hacker. Hacking is essentially multiple fields in one; it isn't enough to merely be an extremely proficient programmer (in fact, in many cases you don't even need to be a good one), Nor is it enough to just have great social skills (more on this later.) To be a hacker means to know multiple disciplines extremely well, and that doesn't come without dedication.

If you're learning to hack, don't expect it to be a weekend project, or even a summer job. It's a difficult task which only a few people in the world have successfully mastered. Because of this, if you're someone that gives up easily, you might want to sleep on hacking as a career.

We'll look at the rest of the things you need to become a hacker later, now, let's check out the three primary kinds of hackers.

Black Hat

Black hat hackers are most of those you see on TV. They are defined as hackers that commit illegal activities for malicious purposes. In layman terms, this is basically just hackers that don't obtain the permission of the people they're hacking beforehand, and do it with an agenda which is self-beneficial. This kind of hacker is well represented in pop culture because they display an excellent villain for the audience. In reality, the life of a black hat hacker tends to be much worse than we see on TV. They're often shown living in mansions, and living a lavish life while the FBI is unable to find them. Fortunately, this isn't quite how it plays out in real life. Black hats tend to get busted, and even those that don't constantly live on edge because there could be an FBI warrant for them at any time.

With that being said, there's one TV trope of black hats that tends to ring true, and that is the one where the black hat hacker gets recruited after serving their time. History has shown that there are countless black hats that, once they've served their sentence, end up working either in the private sector as cybersecurity experts, or cooperate with the government for a hefty paycheck.

For an example of black hat hacking, we don't need to look any further than Behzad Mesri. Behzad conducted reconnaissance of HBO's networks and did things ranging from mundane to outright criminal. Most of his deeds consisted of stealing extensive employee information, as well as taking information from their corporate servers. He also took and shared episodes of some of HBO's most popular shows, leading to the loss of countless dollars.

A bit before OurMine hacked HBO's social media accounts, Mesri sent them a somewhat cocky email, telling them he was in possession of over a terabyte of their data, as well as saying that he had the full scripts of HBO's most popular show - Game of Thrones. Furthermore, he claimed that he had data on some of HBO's shows which hadn't even aired yet.

With this, he threatened the company, asking them for $5.5 million paid to him in BTC, or he would air all of the data to the public. Unfortunately for Mesri, HBO denied his offer, and he began the leaks. He sent statements to the media, as well as publishing his findings via multiple fake Twitter accounts.

This, also, didn't pan out quite as planned. Law enforcement in the US found the Iranian hacker to be guilty of wire fraud, computer hacking, and attempt to undermine confidentiality. The total of all of these charges could cost Mesri over 20 years of his life behind bars. With this, came a federal arrest warrant, however, fortunately for him he managed to escape.

There has been no news concerning Mesri ever since then. The FBI presumes that he fled to his native country of Iran. Due to the US's less than ideal relations with Iran, it's quite likely that Mesri will never need to stand trial for his crimes.

This is a case of a black hat that, at first glance, looks successful. After all, he did hack into HBO right? Well, it was a successful hack, however, it didn't quite pan out the way Mesri wanted, as he's now left without a single cent in BTC, as well as being unable to visit any country that's allied with the United States because he'd be risking his life.

This is quite a common case for black hat hackers that live in countries that are at war, or close to. With that being said, if Iran and the US manage to get to a successful relationship, Mesri could once again find his life in danger.

White Hat

White hat hackers are the distinct opposite of black hats (shocker, right?) because they hack in the interest of their employer. Their purpose is to find exploits and weaknesses in the network and fix them before a black hat is able to abuse them. In TV shows, you've probably seen these being referred to as "counter hackers," but this is only partly true. While it is accurate that white hats are usually employed to counter black hats, they very rarely get into typing-intensive real-time battles. It's much more akin to holding down a fort. If the black hat can find a way that nobody knows about beneath the castle, they win; if they can't, the white hat wins.

In reality, most of the time, you'll find that the job of the white hat hacker is a lot harder than the black hat. Using the same castle metaphor, it takes hundreds of people to build it, but only one maniac with a bomb to blow it up. With that being said, there is a certain amount of overlap between the white hat hacker and the black hat hacker. Both of these hackers are fundamentally looking for the same thing - holes in the network's security. This is why so many black hats eventually transfer to white hats, and actually do really well for themselves.

It's extremely important to keep in mind that the job of a white hat hacker is a lot more time-intensive than the job of a black hat. A black hat hacker can easily live off of one very successful hack, while the white hat is often paid on a per-contract or per-hour basis, and only the superstars of the white hat world would be able to do such a thing. Despite this, white hat hacking comes with an excellent perk - you won't spend half your life behind bars because of it, and ain't that great?

White hat hacking is also a lot less lonesome. While black hat hackers have their groups, they're usually filled with tension. After all, you usually don't want anyone else to exploit an error that you found before you do, because you'd be losing out on money/fame. This makes these groups more useful for making organized attacks, rather than being a group of coworkers. In the white hat hacking world, you'll be working much more closely with other white hat hackers. This leads to a much better quality of life, because you can have coworkers, as well as regular working hours.

Another great thing about being a white hat hacker is that you get to do what you find fun for money. Most hackers don't start out aspiring to make tons of money, they simply have fun finding insecurities in software and getting into them. The white hat hacker is actually able to do this legally, rather than needing to conceal their presence like the black hat, they can put their name out in public. The road of a white hat hacker is also much better if you're looking for fame. While black hat hackers often get famous, this is usually quite a bit after getting arrested, and there isn't much point to it after that, now is there? On the other hand, white hat hackers can get famous much easier, and while the general public will rarely know of them, the field of cybersecurity is broad enough you'll still have people coming up to you on the street.

As for an example of both a white hat hacker, as well as a black hat hacker turned white hat, we need to look no further than one of the most famed hackers that have ever lived - Kevin Mitnick.

Kevin is most likely the most famous white (also called ethical) hacker in the world. This is partly due to the fact that his story is not merely one of success, but one of redemption. He was not always the most ethical hacker around the block, shall we say?

Over 20 years ago, in 1995, Kevin got into a run-in with the law. Eventually, his arrest even made national news in the United States. Such a high-profile arrest is very rare for computer crimes even today, and it was almost unheard of back then. He was chased by law enforcement for his two and a half year series of attacks, where he displayed his hacking skills in front of the whole world. One of his black hat "projects" was breaching security in a company titled the Digital Equipment Corporation. Let's just say that wasn't the best publicity for a tech company, shall we?

Once he was inside of their system, he proceeded to copy most of the software that he found. For this, he was arrested and imprisoned in 1988, however, this did not stop Mitnick in the slightest. He had a supervised release, but even before he was done with his punishment, he had been at it again. That time, he decided to hack into the Pacific Bell voice mail systems and he succeeded. He did this by using techniques such as intercepting passwords, and he has since advocated for using a mixture of real-life and digital tactics for this.

It's no secret that if you violate what is essentially parole, you'll end up with a rougher sentence. Mitnick got another 22 months added onto his already 46-month long sentence purely for violating supervision. Afterward, he was once again released after serving his sentence, in full this time. Mitnick felt that he had done enough on the "dark side" of the hacking world. This led to him deciding to be a white hat hacker after getting out of prison. Naturally, Mitnick's fame as a black hat hacker started a global frenzy, after all, who wouldn't want such a famous guy to be their own consultant? Turns out, not many fortune 500 companies skimped on enlisting Mitnick's aid for outrageous sums of money.

Heck, even the FBI itself sought out Mitnick in order to have him help them out with their work. Naturally, this was also accompanied by another hefty paycheck.

Because of this, Mitnick has become somewhat of an icon in the white hat world. He has also written multiple best-selling books, as well as holding speeches which have been attended by thousands of people worldwide.

Once he donned the white hat, Mitnick also began to teach his skills to others. He led social engineering classes, as well as teaching people some of the most state-of-the-art penetration testing methods.

Grey Hat

Grey hat hackers exist somewhere in the middle between white and black hats (figures, right?)

To put it simply, grey hat hackers are either white hats that also break the law, or black hats that are not doing it for malicious/personal purposes. At first, this might sound a bit confusing, and, well, it is. Many people argue that the distinction of "grey hat" shouldn't even exist. After all, if black hat hackers were those that broke the law, and white hats those that followed it, wouldn't it be much simpler? Well, while that would indeed increase the simplicity of the hacking world, it would not help much when defining what one does.

Let's look at the first way to be a grey hat hacker - being a white hat hacker that breaks the law.

If a white hat hacker is one that abides by laws while also providing assistance to companies/the government within ethical bounds, then a grey hat hacker in this sense would be one that breaks the law to do the same thing. For example, let's say you see a glaring error in a company's code, but you don't work for them. If you were this kind of grey hat, you would hack into the company, not do anything, and then show them a fix for all of their issues.

In this case, you broke the law - you hacked the company without their permission, after all. On the other hand, it would be difficult, if not impossible, to argue that your actions weren't ethical. This kind of white hat hacker is much like a vigilante in today's world. They serve an ethical purpose, despite not getting to it by legal means, this can often be because the legal means are too slow, or the hacker just doesn't trust them.

This kind of hacker can be thought of as either a black hat or a white hat hacker. After all, if you think hacking should be divided by whether the action is ethical or not, then it's a white hat, but if you think it should be done by legality, then it is a black hat hack. If you take into consideration both moral value and legality, then it falls in the middle - a grey hat.

The other kind of grey hat hacker is one that does things illegally, but doesn't do it for any kind of malicious purpose. You'll have probably encountered many of these on TV shows. In D&D terms, they are the chaotic neutrals of the world. The Joker-like characters. Usually, a grey hacker will break the law and hack into sites not for any personal gain, but simply for sport. Basically, a grey hat hacker like this will simply be pursuing entertainment, rather than a concrete agenda.

Personally, I'd put these closer to the black hat side of the spectrum. This is mostly because, well, they're doing illegal things without benefiting the populace at all. They're not benefiting anyone but themselves. Sure, they aren't explicitly hurting anyone, but neither is jaywalking most of the time, and it's still a crime. Doing an exploit on a company's site can easily have negative consequences for them.

Now, in this batch of grey hackers, it's debatable whether or not those that hack for fame fall in. After all, fame is a selfish motivation that doesn't explicitly hurt anyone in and of itself. On the other hand, the road to fame is often paved with theft and destruction. After all, who would you remember, the guy that hacked into your favorite TV network and deleted everything, and stole their money, or the guy that hacked into it "for the lols" and then did absolutely nothing with it?

Now, when it comes to hacker relations, usually you'll find that white hats hate black hats and vice versa. It is much like the relationship between criminals and cops in real life - they don't like each other much. On the other hand, grey hats are generally disliked to a much lesser extent, however, they will commonly be looked down upon in hacker communities due to being perceived as lacking either a moral or ideological compass. All in all, much like most online communities, there's quite a bit of toxicity in public hacking forums, although private groups are a different story, and tend to be rather nice places.

There are two further kinds of hackers that are defined separately from the ethics-legality axis of the "hats" and those are:

Script Kiddie

You'll find this term thrown around the internet a lot. A "Script Kiddie" is a person (usually an adolescent, or teenager) that has no technical skills, but rather uses ready-made programs for their hacks. While many hackers will sometimes incorporate their own methods alongside pre-made programs, script kiddies are usually looked down upon in the hacking community. You'll find this mostly being used as either an insult, or a poster explaining that they're a beginner. It is worth noting that being a "script kiddie" doesn't actually mean you write your own scripts. This can get quite confusing to newbies on the scene, as despite having "script" in the name, all they do is take other people's scripts and use them for their own purposes, often messing up in the process.

Most people start out as a script kiddie, however, that is generally an area you don't want to stick around in for long. Your skills won't get any better from learning a few programs that someone else made, or learning how to recite simple Linux scripts off the top of your head. Hackers need to constantly be honing their skills, because otherwise the rampantly evolving field of cybersecurity will eclipse us and leave us in the dust-a death sentence for any hacker.

It's also good to know that almost all Script Kiddies are black hats. After all, nobody is going to employ you to use a pre-existing program. Because of this, they're looked down even more, as black hat hackers are generally those with more hacking skill, and those that have a much more difficult time of gaining resources (there's no black hat hacker university, last I checked.)

A good example of a Script Kiddie is...well...me, most people start out as a script kiddie in order to impress their friends. Such was the case for me, I would run around my elementary school bragging how I got into this or that site. Of course, I always neglected to mention that I was using pre-existing tools and that I was only able to affect the front-end of the website. A get-rich-quick scheme this was not, as the front end of sites usually doesn't exactly contain much valuable information. By the time I got into high school, I started to be embarrassed by my script kiddie past, and decided to bury it completely. The thing with script kiddies is that they're usually teens that want to be popular among their peers for one reason or another, and they see hacking as a clever avenue to get to that. They also don't have the pre-existing knowledge, nor the willingness to learn it in order to actually perform successful hacks themselves without using tools.

Oftentimes, like it was the case for me, script kiddies will eventually learn how to hack "for real" as in, how to look for holes in security themselves, and learning how "proper" exploits work in reality. Unfortunately, there are also people that don't grow out of this, and they wind up at the office bragging about what kind of site they got into this time.

Hacktivists

Hacktivists are a unique breed, personally, I'd consider them grey hats most of the time. They are basically "hacking activists" (hence the name) and they hack in order to show an agenda. These hacks will range from a hardcore black hat (DDoS-ing a site, or deleting their data in order to show a point.) To pretty much white hat (hacking into deep web pedophilia circles and exposing them to the world.)

These hackers exist everywhere on the black-white hat spectrum. This is what makes it quite difficult to write about them. The only worthwhile thing to mention here is that they do all they do for an agenda. Generally, hacktivist groups will be much like the hippies of the post-war era. They'll be against war, for democracy etc. However, their methods can be rather varied in reality.

Hacktivists also often operate in groups, rather than working as lone hackers. This is because they're hacking for an agenda, and people of the same ideology will often unite under a single banner. This is potentially one of the most dangerous kinds of hacking, as a group of hacktivists working for the wrong agenda can wreak havoc on certain parts of society.

A great, and extremely popular example of hacktivism is the popular hacking group "Anonymous."

Now, many people will argue on whether or not Anonymous counts as a hacktivist group. This is due to their size, which is quite large, and a lot of their members joined without truly believing in the ideals. On the other hand, this is a natural consequence of any ideological organization getting larger, so I've chosen to use them as our example.

You can look at hacktivism as the most high-tech mode of protest. Savvy programmers from all around the world united under the single banner of Anonymous. The signature of the Anonymous organization is the famous Guy Fawkes mask, they've been pulling attack after attack on a variety of targets. The main things they elected to fight for was decentralization, peace, and democracy. While there is media controversy about whether or not they're truly standing just for that, at least according to the general populace, they're somewhat admirable figures. Like most hacktivists, Anonymous is very polarizing; you either love them or you hate them.

Now let's look at some of their most famous attacks:

The first time Anonymous became an international media sensation was back in 2008; this was led against the Scientologist Church in a very long project titled Project Chanology. Not liking where this was headed, Anonymous decided that this project wouldn't fly. They hacked into the Scientology Churches networks, and flooded their fax machines with straight-up jet black ink. This, together with an (at the time) new method called "Google bombing" resulted in significant damage to the Church/cult. Google bombing is a means of tarnishing one's reputation by making Google associate it with negative terms such as, in this case, rape, cult, evil, dangerous etc. This is done by basically spamming Google with searches connecting the two.

The Chanology Project was the hacker group's response to the Church of Scientology using the internet itself as a means of censoring information, and spreading misinformation about the exact things that they do. As an example of this, the church claimed a copyright notice against YouTube, because one of their propaganda videos wound up on the popular streaming service.

In this video, Tom Cruise, who is actually a very high-profile Scientologist was shown extolling the values that the church of Scientology holds in a manner that many people looking at the video deemed to be either brainwashed or delusional. A scandal ensued.

Anonymous posted the video again, after the lawsuit, and made a call-to-action, calling out the people of the world to not only speak out against the church of Scientology, but truly do something about their immoral actions.

Since this exposure, the hacker group gained international fame and renown. Unsurprisingly, the church of Scientology had very many haters, but at the same time, this opened the door for some more controversial hacks. But first, one of the actions why Anonymous is most idolized.

A few years ago, the group gained international acceptance, for a time at least, after participating in a massive crackdown on child pornography. Anonymous alone led to the shutdown of over 40 illegal child porn websites, mostly found in the deep web. Certain Anonymous members found caches of some of the sites while going through a site on the deep web called the Hidden Wiki. To put it simply, the Hidden Wiki is like a directory for dubiously legal websites that exist on the deep web. These sites are invisible to traditional search engines like

Google or Bing, but to the members of Anonymous, they were as clear as day.

The first website they took down was the biggest one, Lolita City, one of the biggest child porn sites in history fell that day. It was a platform made for pedophiles to share pictures, videos, and audio clips of child pornography. Later on, Anonymous decided to publish the list of the site's 1589 members publicly. This operation, which they appropriately named Operation Darknet went beyond what even the world's most prestigious agencies were able to do. Furthermore, it increased awareness of the deep and dark web for the people of the world.

This was yet another act of hacktivism for which Anonymous was praised for, but as we're about to see, they didn't restrict their activities merely to digital criminals.

The next hack that they did happened to the San Francisco Bay Area Rapid Transit system, aka. BART. BART had decided to turn off subterranean cell phone service, in order to help kill the protests which were scheduled for their platforms on that very day. The protest was held because there was a shooting of an innocent, unarmed man by the BART police only a month before that. The civilians had planned to stop the trains from running, however, without the ability to coordinate together, their plans quickly fell apart.

In a world without hacktivists, this act of censorship would've simply flown by. After all, who can do anything about it? Well, Anonymous, being people that could do something about it, decided to take up the mantle. After BART's attempt at censorship, there was immediate outcry started by the media. Quickly after this, Anonymous started attacking. The first thing they did was crack (get in) their user database found on their consumer-oriented website "MyBART.org," there, they decided to post the names, emails, as well as ZIP codes and passwords of a variety of users of the site. Together with this, they wrote and published a manifesto which explained that the company had decided to violate a fundamental human right- the right to assemble and protest. Afterward, they decided to hack into the BART police department's websites, and then they posted the names and emails of a variety of officers in the Bay Area.

They also took it upon themselves to organize multiple protests, in the image of the first one which BART had managed to stifle in the few weeks after that event.

Finally, when BART didn't believe that this was a mistake, and their spokesman, Linton Johnson, refused to apologize, Anonymous took a slightly pettier route, and decided to attack the man on an emotional level, posting nude pictures of him online.

This hack is much more controversial than the last two. Obviously, the intentions themselves were good, however, the actions themselves were a lot more debatable. While hacking into sites and making them stop working would likely be seen as an appropriate response to BART's actions, revealing private information of its users sent alarms ringing through the heads of many Anonymous supporters. Furthermore, a public attack on a spokesman by means of sharing their nude pictures was not seen kindly by most people.

Especially controversial was the release of information on police officers. After all, they're merely people doing their jobs, are they not? Furthermore, it would not be hard to imagine a world where after getting out of jail, a criminal goes to take revenge on an officer. This is seen by many as a case of

Anonymous becoming much closer to what they're trying to fight against, violating people's right to privacy.

The next hack we'll be going over has been affectionately referred to as "Cybergate", and happened back in February 2011. Aaron Barr, the CEO of a cybersecurity company titled HBGary Federal, wanted to reveal some of the information he had about his members at a conference. Now, this kind of breach of privacy didn't sit well with many in the world and among them were the hackers of Anonymous.

First, they went into HBGary's site and decided to replace the homepage with a logo of theirs, as well as stating that they are not to be trifled with. A mild digression here is that this started the trend of script kiddies and other hacker groups putting their banners on sites they "conquered." Anonymous is a good example of good intentions that sometimes go awry, even if not by their own making.

After this, Anonymous was still not satisfied. They went after their phones, and took over 70 thousand messages off of their email system. Not only that, but they went as far as creating a database for these emails online. In fact, they even made it searchable! They also posted all of this, together, on the Twitter account of Mr. Barr...which they also decided to hack.

These emails contained within a variety of messages which would greatly harm the companies public image. The whistleblower website WikiLeaks is, even today, hailed as one of the most influential sites of the 21st century. Well, Barr had his plans to cripple it by using cyberattacks and disinformation campaigns. Fortunately, Anonymous got the cyberattack idea first. Barr's emails also showed that a law firm called Hunton & Williams, famous for its operations against WikiLeaks was employed by the US Chamber of

Commerce. It was revealed that the US government was hiring these organizations to have them attack those entities (like Wikileaks) that they found were harmful to them. After this, there was an extensive government investigation on a lot of these companies, ending with a variety of jailings.

This hack was also generally looked upon as positive, however, there were some downsides. It started a so-called "Anonymous craze" where many people called themselves members of the Anonymous, or aspired to be hackers. Many of these went on to become black hat hackers, missing Anonymous' peaceful agenda, and seeing only the fame and destruction that followed in their wake. As we've already said, it also sparked the trend of hacking groups leaving their marks upon websites. This led to quite a few black-hat organizations being busted, due to getting too cocky. By today, most people have understood that outside of hacktivist organizations, leaving one's banner on top of a hacked site is only looking for trouble.

The final hack we'll be looking over is of a different nature. Anonymous was, up until this point, merely messing around with private companies, and whistleblowing public organizations. Our next hack discusses something a lot more serious; we are, of course, talking about the Arab Spring.

The Arab Spring was a series of anti-government protests in Syria. These ranged from people parading in the streets to screaming and assaulting officials. Anonymous, too, played a part in the Arab uprisings. They did a series of illegal DDoS attacks on the websites of three Arab countries, namely, Tunisia, Iran, and Egypt. All of these attacks were using very simple software, pointing perhaps that it was a less-skilled branch of Anonymous doing the job. However, due to these countries never being on the sharp end of cyber warfare before, they worked. The websites of all three countries crashed.

There were also some more significant hacks ongoing at the same time. The hackers of Anonymous ended up showing the world the emails and passwords of many officials which decided to go against the protests. This attack was much more organized and clever, they also got information from not three, but four countries this time. All of this was released together for the public to see.

After this came perhaps the most dangerous of the hacks. Anonymous hacked Syria's defense ministry website. The website itself was replaced with a simple, but a meaningful picture. It was a symbol of the democratic movement which was burning across Syria, called the pre-Ba'athist flag. This was intended as a message of intense support for the movement made by the Syrian populace. It also called upon Syrian soldiers to act on what they knew was right and go to protect the protesters fighting for everyone's rights.

What Anonymous Left Behind

Anonymous still continues to hack today. The last full-blown major hack associated with them was in 2017, and was something of a Darknet part 2, with Anonymous hacking into yet another batch of child porn sites.

This is less important; what we want to talk about here is what the Anonymous left behind. Whether their legacy was good or bad. This is important to know because, if one day, you were to become a hacktivist, it would be your responsibility to take care of the legacy you leave in your wake. If it is good, then excellent, however, as we'll soon see, not all that Anonymous left behind them was a good thing.

Firstly, they were pretty much the progenitors of the hacktivist movement. They showed the world that even in this age of bullets and bombs, the populace could still rise up against their country by using their own tools. In this case, the tools were pieces of code and digital devices. The excellent thing about this is that it opened a whole new avenue of government protest. At this point, when a company, or even the government itself, makes an anti-populace announcement, they are at risk of facing cyberattacks.

One of their remnants which wasn't good or bad was the rise of awareness of hacking. Due to their nature as a non-government affiliated hacktivist organization, it is only natural that the government spread misinformation about Anonymous. You soon found evil hackers on TV playing bad guys for hacking the government for one reason or another. With that being said, the Anonymous simultaneously represented hope, a goal, and a fantasy for aspiring hackers of the day. After all, if they can affect the whole world with merely their hacking knowledge at their disposal, why couldn't you do it too?

Another leftover was the increase in cybersecurity around the world. The field of cybersecurity barely existed until it was shown that it was absolutely necessary. After all, even if Anonymous were, fundamentally, a people-loving organization, who is to say all groups of people that can hack are going to be the same? After all, if the Anonymous managed to hack into a military site, what's stopping an equally capable, but much more malicious group from launching weapons at a neighboring country? Because of this, governments around the world started to employ cybersecurity experts in their ranks.

This trend extended to private companies as well. After all, nobody wanted to be the next company to get hacked by a hacktivist group and have their website be caricatured. Worse yet, no CEO wanted nude pictures of them to be available freely on the internet.

Another legacy left behind them, not at all positive, was the idea that hacking private sites and releasing said information was somehow "okay." In a way, Anonymous is to blame for many of today's black hat hacking organizations. They demonstrated what an organized group of hacking experts could do. Is it really a surprise that some of the people that know how to hack weren't as philanthropic as they were?

This looming danger is still present today. Fortunately, no such groups have emerged, and the worst that has happened has been malicious hacks ending in either property damage, or loss of monetary wealth, neither of which is bad to the point of causing a war.

What Do I Need to Become A Hacker?

Becoming a hacker isn't easy and, as we've talked at the start of this chapter, you'll need a huge amount of determination and decisiveness. This isn't a line of work you can enter without a dose of hard work. With that being said, there are quite a few things which you'll need in order to become a quality hacker.

First of all, you'll need a computer ... or will you? While in the past, saying you'll need a computer might have been true, these days hacking without a computer is possible, if not recommended. It's theoretically possible to be able to hack off of your phone, it just isn't done very often as computers are a lot more practical. On the other hand, using some low-tech means can be a nice change of pace sometimes.

Next, you'll need a proper operating system. Again, it's technically possible to be a successful hacker off of Windows, however, it simply isn't very advisable. You need to know how to deal with UNIX based operating systems (So MAC or Linux) because UNIX systems are the systems on which most internet machines are run. While you can access the internet without running a UNIX based operating system, you can't really be that successful of a hacker without at least a broad understanding of it. This understanding is much easier to attain by working with one yourself, rather than simply studying off of the internet. Furthermore, you need an operating system which gives you a lot of freedom. Unfortunately for the Apple lovers out there, Apple doesn't give much freedom. In fact, iOS is probably the most restrictive operating system out there today. This is why we recommend a Linux-based operating system, rather than any others. We'll look over why we're picking Linux over alternatives, as well as the kinds of Linux we recommend in the next chapter.

Next, you'll need to know HTML. While this book doesn't teach it (it's too complex of a thing to put in an introductory book like this.) HTML is essentially the markup language that determines how things like text are displayed online. It's not very difficult to learn, and there's a variety of books and tutorials available out there today which will easily teach you HTML.

Now, after this you'll want to learn how to script. We'll be talking about this in chapter 3, which will introduce you to the world of Scripting and teach you exactly how to do it. Now, we'll be only giving you some rudimentary, introductory scripts. You'll want to familiarize yourself with scripting a lot more than what we've presented here, however, we'll offer you an excellent starting point to continue your education off of. Scripting is the backbone of every hacker's skillset. This is why you should make sure to learn it.

The next thing you'll want to learn is a popular programming language like, say, Java or C++, alternatively C# or any of its alternatives will do the job just as well. This is the part of hacking that most aspiring hackers look up to. As a hacker, you'll likely be writing a metric ton of code every day. After all, pretty much everything, not just on the internet, but on computers and all digital devices runs on code. Because of this, you'll need to make sure that you know the basics of many of the world's most popular programming languages. After all, you can't crack what you don't know.

Python is an excellent language to start with. It doesn't have the immense learning curve that a language like Java or C++ does, but is used a lot all the same. Python is used all around the internet as both a front end and back end language. Because of this, you won't be losing out on anything by learning it. Quite the contrary, one could argue that learning Python is more beneficial to your hacking career than learning a language like Java is. My personal recommendation would be Python if you've got a thing for programming, be it experience or just a lot of time. On the other hand, if you're pressed for time, or simply completely new to all this I'd recommend you go for Ruby. This is because the language has been skyrocketing in popularity lately, and even more than that, it basically reads like English. It's an extremely simple language from a syntax standpoint (as in, its syntax is simple to read.) On the other hand, it has potential that's close to C++ and Java when it comes to programming in general. It's also an excellent language to know if you switch from hacking to a more mainstream career.

Next, you'll need creativity. A lot of hacking might seem like brute-force work where you just type away at a keyboard, set up some protective measures if you're a white hat, or set up a botnet if you're a black hat, and then just let it be. Oftentimes, this trade can be like that, especially if you're working as a cybersecurity expert for a company that isn't very successful. On the other hand, if you've got a more difficult employer, they won't be satisfied with run of the mill measures. Keep in mind that black hats are quite creative in their approach. When you're penetration testing, you can't just check against a normal DDoS attack, you need to check if any users have too many permissions, because, for example, a black hat hacker could've gone through your rubbish bin and found their password. It's not very easy to account for all the things that black hats could do as a cybersecurity expert. This makes your job all the more difficult. You have to get in the mindset of not just any old black hat hacker, but a good and creative one.

Problem-solving skills are probably the most underrated part of the hacker skillset. A lot of people think of hackers as merely a subset of programmers, and to a degree, they're right. You won't get many places as a hacker without at least some programming skills, and your programming skills will be average at best without some problem-solving ability. These days, white hat hackers at many of the world's top organizations are hired using tests that incorporate essentially acting as a black hat hacker does. You'll be tasked with breaching the security of a site very often. This requires a lot of problem solving and attention to detail, as you'll need to identify holes in the companies' code and successfully exploit them. On the job, you'll also need to learn how to solve programming problems, and how to make fool-proof code.

An internet connection is also pretty necessary for hacking. You won't be doing any hacking of websites if you can't access them in the first place. Surprisingly, you don't need some extra-good connection that can run NASA's internet needs on it. All you need is a moderately good internet connection for most of the things you'll be doing. On the other hand, there are some hacks that incorporate a much higher bandwidth, so if you want to err on the side of safety, you might as well get an excellent one.

Surprisingly enough, another very good skill to have as a hacker is social skills. You might think of hacking as a solitary thing in the world. Hackers in popular culture are represented as antisocial geeks after all, aren't they? Well, even if they're represented like that, there have been many hackers in history who have gained access to sites using much more down to earth means. There have been methods such as rummaging through rubbish bins, as well as posing as employees, or making pretend phone calls saying how you've forgotten your password. If you're planning to be a grey hat, or a hacktivist, then social skills will be an extremely important part of your skillset. This goes double for hacktivists, who need to have a good social presence so that they can deliver their ideals more efficiently to the people. Even white hats need social skills to a degree, although in a different way. You want to be well-liked by your coworkers much like any other job, and making positive relations with them will make your job much easier to do. It's also a lot easier to get a job in the first place if you've been brushing up on your social skills lately.

That's it! These are the things you'll be needing on your road as a hacker. You might've noticed that there's a bunch of things on there, and while that's true, you can afford to drop one or two most of the time, and still be a successful hacker. On the other hand, if you can manage to combine all of them, you've got a bright future ahead of you!

Chapter 2: Why Linux?

Linux this, Linux that. By now, you're probably quite annoyed at my constant mentioning of the operating system as the be-all-end-all of hacking operating systems, however, I swear I have valid reasons for this. In this chapter, we'll be looking at all of the reasons why you should be using Linux as opposed to any of its competition when it comes to hacking. There are quite a few, ranging from ideological, to monetary.

This chapter will also discuss which distribution you should be running, as well as the basics of Linux.

What Is Linux?

Linux is an operating system that has been powering a wide range of applications, ranging from phones to supercomputers around the world, ever since the mid-'90s. Today, Linux has a userbase that spans across the globe, and is by far the biggest out of any open-source operating system.

The Android phone operating system (you know, the 1st or 2nd most popular one in the world, depending on who you ask?) Was also made taking inspiration from Linux, in fact, there are many Linux distributions far more different from each other than from Android.

Today, Linux is what most of the Internet is run on, in addition to all of the top 500 supercomputers in the whole world. Heck, even the global stock exchange is run on Linux.

The operating system that we call Linux is actually not all one piece. In fact, Linux is segmented into many different parts, each with a different purpose. This is quite useful, as it lets people customize their own installation of Linux without affecting every part of the operating system.

The different parts of Linux are as follows:

The Bootloader is a piece of software that is tasked with managing all of the processes which occur when your computer starts up, also referred to as "boot processes." Now, usually this is just a screen that pops up and goes away, it doesn't look very flashy, but without it, nothing else would function (plus you can modify it to give you some pretty sick visuals.)

The Init system is a sub-system that is tasked with bootstrapping the user space and controls all of the daemons installed on the system. Now, these are quite optional, and there's a lot of strife in the Linux world over which, and if they should be used. The most popular one is systemd, however, it is also the most controversial. Usually, it manages the process of booting up after the bootloader has done all it needs to do.

Graphical servers are mere subsystems displaying things on your monitor. Yes, that means everything you see on your monitor is a simple subsystem, these graphical servers are often called "X".

The Kernel is a bit confusing. See, many people refer to the kernel as Linux and it is pretty much the heart of the operating system - the most basic, fundamental level. It is tasked with looking at memory, other devices you implement, and the CPU and GPU operation.

Daemons are subsystems of Init systems, they are controlled by Init systems and are usually working just on services that run in the background. For example, printing and sound will usually be tackled by separate daemons.

The desktop environment is where you spend, well, most of your time. As a user, this is where you're supposed to spend all of your time on Linux. It contains everything you could possibly interact with. While there are many to choose from, ranging from GNOME (the most popular one) to more underground ones like Pantheon, all of them have the same base apps, like file managers and basic web browsers/games.

Applications are everything else that we haven't mentioned so far. Do you know that new browser you installed? It's an application. How about that pack-fresh AAA game title? Yup, you guessed it, it's also an application. To be short, applications are everything that doesn't come pre-installed with your operating system. You'll find that most distributions of Linux come with some sort of tool that makes downloading applications off of the internet much easier. The Ubuntu distribution, for example, has its own application store, much like the Android app store which lets you look across thousands of applications made for Ubuntu.

What Benefits Does Linux Have?

While this book is geared towards hacking, we cannot neglect the pros and cons of using Linux. After all, it's not very likely you won't use your PC for anything other than hacking. Chances are, you're already used to some operating system, whether it be iOS or Windows. So, what does Linux hold for you that they don't?

Let's begin with a question; do you remember your PC ever having a virus? Chances are, you've been infected a few times. How about slowdowns? Has your OS ever updated and lead to your system slowing down in a way you swore was manufactured? Have software updates ever caused massive computer-wide errors that lead to you having to take it to a repair shop?

Well, let's just say there's a good reason that the top 500 supercomputers in the world run on Linux. The biggest of those reasons is sturdiness. Linux is incredibly reliable at what it does. It doesn't suffer from issues with viruses, nor is there a company behind it that will try to milk your money with scummy business practices.

The next pro is, it's free. As in, you don't have to pay a single cent to install Linux on as many computers as you'd like. 1 computer is as free as 100. So, for example, while a Windows Server 2019 is over $800 USD retail, you'll find that it doesn't even include all licenses you need. For example, you might need a database, or a mail server. Well, all of those will be charged separately. Do you need to add more users? Well, then be prepared to shell out a lot more cash.

So, how does this compare to the Linux server? Well, if you wanted to get all the licenses you need, as well as the latest Linux distribution on a given amount of computers...it would cost you precisely $0. Even if you're making a full-blown server together with a database and everything else, all you'll need is a bit of clever command usage and you're ready to go. This is why you'll find most commercial servers to not be running on Windows, but rather relying on Linux for all their needs.

Alright, maybe you don't care about the cost? You're mister bling-bling and have no issues with money whatsoever. Well, usually you'll find that with wealth comes a need for security and hassle-free experiences. How many times have you had to stop using your PC because of a Windows/iOS update that you had absolutely no way of stopping? If you're anything like I was, the answer is many. On the other hand, Linux will never hassle you with this. It isn't strange for a Linux-based server to make it through many years without ever suffering a reboot.

This means that you can simply sit back and not worry about a thing. Sure, viruses technically exist, and they pop up here and there, but they're tackled much more quickly than on other operating systems, this is partly due to the next thing Linux has on most other mainstream operating systems.

This is the fact that it is open source. We'll delve deeper into this further on in this chapter, when we're looking at Linux from a hacking perspective. For now, it's enough for you to know that this means anyone can take, use and modify any of the code that Linux runs on, creating their own version.

How To Install Linux

At first, holding to the idea of installing a brand new operating system might seem incredibly frightening. After all, if you haven't used any operating systems other than the one you're using right now, how will you get used to it? Will you even be able to perform the installation?

Now, you'll want to decide whether or not you want to dual boot. Dual-booting refers to the act of using two operating systems simultaneously, which is to say that when you're booting up your PC, you'll be able to pick which one you go to. This way, you could have an operating system you're used to for your day to day needs, and one Linux installation for every time you want to hack. Keep in mind that dual booting is fairly taxing on the PC. It can be a mess to get working, and even when it isn't it'll definitely slow you down. You'll also need to have quite a bit of memory, as both operating systems will be taking up space. All in all, I don't advise dual booting though if you absolutely will not let go of your pet operating system then it may be the only available choice out there.

For a lot of folks out there, it might seem like dual booting is the only option, however, it's worth keeping in mind that

Linux is actually an incredibly easy to use operating system. Now, with this comes yet another surprise; Linux, despite all of its complexity on the inside, is actually one of the easiest operating systems to get going. A great thing about Linux is that most distributions offer a Live distribution. What this means is that it's enough to put the operating system on a disk or USB drive to run it. This means that you don't need to immediately delete the operating system you've been using before. You get all of Linux's functions without ever needing to say bye to your operating system, although it is a lot slower, so I advise using this only for trial purposes. So, let's say you've tried Linux out, and that you really like it, now you'll want to install it. Usually, this is as simple to do as clicking the "install" button, and following instructions of the installation wizard.

Now, usually there will be a few steps to this. After all, no matter how simple it is, you're still downloading a new operating system. There are a few things you'll need to ensure before you start installing your Linux distribution, and they are:

First of all, you'll want to make sure that the PC you're putting Linux on actually supports Linux, or simply put, meets its requirements. Now, you'll find that pretty much any PC that isn't a literal toaster (though some of those might be able to.) Is able to support Linux, hence this usually isn't much of a concern. This part of the installation process will also commonly ask whether or not you want to package any third-party software together with your installation. To save yourself the hassle, you might as well get a music and video player so you don't have to get one later on.

Generally, you'll find that it's an excellent idea to be connected to the internet while you do this. Keep in mind that it is not necessary to have a wireless connection at the ready while downloading Linux, though it can be helpful. If you've got one handy then it'll make it much easier, as pretty much all third-party apps will need to be downloaded off of the internet, rather than being on the Live CD/USB themselves.

Now you'll need to check your hard drive space. If your hard drive is too full to put Linux on it, then you can't, it's as simple as that. Obviously, that is unless you're willing to say goodbye to some of the content you've got there. Now, presuming you've got enough drive space for the operating system, the installation window will usually ask you how you'd like to install Linux. This is where the fabled dual booting question comes into play. If you're planning to dual boot, make two partitions on your HDD for your two operating systems. If not, just let Linux install over the whole hard drive. If you end up wanting to switch to a different distribution of Linux, this category will also usually hold the option to update your current distro, or change to a brand new one.

After that, you'll be facing some of the rudimentary questions that make your life easier. Most installation windows will have you pick your location so that they can easier guess the language that you want your system in. Afterward, they'll be inclined to check the layout of your keyboard, and finally, you'll be asked to set up a user account by giving it a username and a password.

After this, all that is left is to reboot your system and enjoy Linux. It is really that easy, and requires no more setup than this. Some games require more setup than Linux. Now that we're done with that, let's go back to hacking, and check out some reasons why a hacker might want to use this operating system for their needs.

It's Open Source

I've already mentioned it, but unlike the other mainstream operating systems Linux works on an Open Source basis. That means that the operating system is available to anyoone, anytime, for free and they're free to modify and distribute their version.

This has led to multiple Linux distributions being made for hacking purposes. After all, if people use Linux to hack, it shouldn't be a surprise when they make whole distributions out of it.

Linux Has Transparency

One of the fundamental tenets of hacking is that you have to have a good understanding of your operating system. To a smaller, but still significant extent, you want to know the operating system of whoever you're attacking as well. Fortunately, Linux is 100% transparent, meaning you can not only see all of its inner workings, but also play with them to grasp the concepts better.

This isn't exactly the case with other operating systems, who aren't as happy as Linux to let you look under their hood. For example Windows tries really hard to prevent you from figuring out how to actually use their operating system to hack. Since it tries so hard to prevent you from knowing what's going on, many aspiring hackers get misinformed and fall into wrong ideas.

Now, we've been talking about distributions all this time, without fully explaining them. Well, put simply, distros, which is short for distributions, are like mini Linux installations which have been made by different people for different things. What this means is that usually you'll find that each distribution of Linux has been specialized for something, whether that be programming, hacking, or general day to day use. So, as a hacker, what are some distributions you might want to consider?

Kali Linux

Kali Linux is by far the most popular hacking-optimized OS out there on the market. It has been made by Offensive Security, and is the rewritten version of BackTrack. It successfully sits on top of this list purely due to the sheer amount of hacking tools that are available on it. It is based on Debian, which makes it a lot easier to use for newcomers that are used to either Windows and Mac, or even the Ubuntu distro of Linux. It comes with over 500 tools for penetration testing already on it, which can help you make your start. Furthermore, the team behind it makes sure that they're always adding new things to these tools, so there's no fear of them becoming outdated. Even better than this, a lot of these tools are on brand new platforms like ARM or even VMware. Kali Linux is also awesome if you're planning to get into digital forensics, as it comes with live boot capability already enabled. This makes it excellent for vulnerability detection right out of the box so to speak.

Parrot Security OS

Parrot Security OS is yet another Linux distro which is based on Debian. It has been developed by Frozenbox's team of professional hackers. This operating system has been designed with cloud friendliness and ethical hacking in mind from the very start. Parrot keeps in mind most of the principles Kali Linux has and applies them, except in a more lightweight package. It's rare to see such an excellent OS for pen testing, cryptography, and other branches of cybersecurity be so lightweight, and even cloud available. This is part of what makes Parrot so efficient to work with, as well as familiar for users of Kali Linux. In reality, Parrot is somewhat of a mutt between Frozenbox's native OS and Kali Linux. Now, if you're an advanced hacker, you'll also appreciate the fact that Parrot is extremely easy to modify on the fly, and has an excellent, supportive community behind it that can get you up to speed on any issues you might have with it.

BackBox

BackBox takes a hint from all the Debian based operating systems we've spoken about so far, and takes it a step further. Backbox takes its roots from the most beginner-friendly Linux distribution of all-Ubuntu. Ubuntu has been hailed as the Windows of the Linux world for almost a decade now, and for good reason. It essentially works better than Windows, while maintaining a similar overall aesthetic. This is what makes Backbox ideal for complete hacking beginners. The operating system itself won't be all too much trouble to use. This is not to say, however, that BackBox has a deficit of good hacking tools written for it, oh no sir. In fact, it has some of the best hacking communities out of all of them. BackBox supports a great variety of tools that have been written for web application analysis, cryptography, and penetration testing in it. It's also quite fast, and is very loved by the hacker community for actually having a desktop environment (most of the distros on this list don't, and rely on you to know commands.)

Samurai Web Testing Framework

Well, the Samurai Web Testing Framework really doesn't leave you with a lot of room to think about what it's for, does it now? It is one of those Linux environments that have been made precisely for one purpose, but lord are they good at that one purpose. The Samurai basically boils down to a Linux environment that has already been configured to operate as a test platform for your web penetration tests. Within this Linux distribution you'll find a variety of hacking tools, and more importantly, tools for detecting vulnerabilities in your own code. If all you care about is Web Penetration Testing, then which distro to get shouldn't really be a question, the Samurai takes the cake on all counts.

Pentoo Linux

Pentoo, despite the silly name, is quite a successful and interesting Linux distro. It is the first one on this list to not be rooted in Debian. Rather, Pentoo takes its roots from the less popular Gentoo Linux. Its scope has also been narrowed down. Fortunately, if an OS which is made simply for penetration testing doesn't really float your boat (can't blame you, everyone needs their computer for more mundane stuff these days.) Then you can install it on top of an already established Gentoo Linux installation. It is also worth noting that Pentoo has a few other quirks, such as being based on XFCE, which by itself comes with a variety of supportive methods that let you save everything you've done before you decide to run off with a USB stick in hand. Some of the tools that this operating system comes from include famous ones like Exploit, Cracker and others. This makes it great for penetration testing, as you can immediately check if you're weak to some of the most common tools on the market.

DEFT Linux

The DEFT Linux installation is one that you don't run into very often. It stands for Digital Evidence And Forensics Toolkit. Once again, it is a case of a narrow distribution which doesn't leave too much room to wonder about its purpose. This Linux distribution has been tailored for one thing, and one thing only, and that is digital forensics. If you're not into it, maybe it simply doesn't appeal to you, or maybe you think it's too hard, whichever the reason, you'll want to sleep on this. It has been built upon Ubuntu, as an extension of DART, which stands for Digital Support Advanced Response Toolkit. It comes ready-made with a variety of popular tools among penetration testers and other IT security professionals, although it is made mostly with forensics in mind.

Caine

This is a distro with absolutely zero black hat potential. Most of the ones we've talked about so far come pre-installed with at least a few tools that could feasibly be used in a black hat fashion. After all, it's hard to conduct penetration tests without something to penetrate. Caine, on the other hand, comes only with database, forensics, and analysis tools which, while making your job easier, won't do much when it comes to testing. This is one of its major weaknesses. However, a major pro of Caine is that it is available on live disk, so you can check it out before ever deciding on whether or not you want to pursue it. Caine stands for Computer-Aided Investigation Environment, and does precisely what it says on the tin.

Network Security Toolkit (NST)

You might have picked up on a trend here, and it's that Linux distro creators aren't very creative when it comes to naming. The Network Security Toolkit is yet another in the series of crimes against interesting names. This is another operating system that isn't based upon Debian, and instead finds its roots in Fedora. The Network Security Toolkit operates on both 32 and 64-bit platforms. The excellent part is that it is also bootable by Live CD, which allows you to use it without fully giving your all to the platform. The bootable CD alone can give you some of the best Network Security software for Linux out there. It has been made mostly with penetration testing in mind, and functions amazingly at this. It's probably the easiest to use, and most beginner-friendly distro to teach you how to do penetration testing (even if it isn't the simplest all-round.) Your x86 system will be made into an ethical hacking monster within minutes of installing the NST on it.

Furthermore, many companies, such as InfoSec offer boot camps for using this software. While many of them are paid, there are also free online courses that will get you up to speed.

BlackArch Linux

Let's give a prize to the first person that correctly names which Linux distribution this one is based on. Ding! We have a winner-it's Arch Linux. Unsurprisingly, BlackArch is its edgier, more useful for hacking cousin. It is probably in the top five of the most popular distributions for ethical hacking in the world, mostly due to the fact that it can be installed over Arch, which is also very popular. You'll find that the ability to essentially run BlackArch on top of Arch isn't all that great for hacking purposes, however, it makes day to day use much easier to manage. So, the moment you install BlackArch you'll be greeted by not just one thousand tools in its codebase, oh no, what you'll be looking at is almost 1500 extensively tested hacking tools, and almost all of them are entirely free. This is an excellent part of using such a widely used hacking OS. The community is blooming, eager to help, and there is a myriad of online tools available to make it better at its job (even though it's already pretty darn great if I do say so myself.)

Bugtraq

Bugtraq isn't so much an operating system, as much as it is an overlay for already-existing operating systems that lets them work a lot better for ethical hacking purposes. This OS is available in the following three "flavors:" Ubuntu, OpenSUSE, and Debian. The development team behind this operating system is already a bit famous for Bugtraq's extremely useful electronic computer security mailing list. Furthermore, it's development team is one hundred percent made up of hackers and cybersecurity professionals. This ensures that

Bugtraq is famous for its electronic mailing list that is purely dedicated to computer security. It is available in Debian, Ubuntu, and OpenSUSE. The Bugtraq developer team consists of experienced hackers and developers that offer a great service for ethical pen testers. It comes with a number of penetration testing tools including mobile forensic tools, malware testing tools and other software developed by the Bugtraq-Community.

Ubuntu

To say the least, putting Ubuntu on this list is controversial. It's not precisely an operating system made for hacking. Well, to be frank, it isn't made for hacking at all. But wait, don't stop reading quite yet, I haven't gone crazy or anything yet, I still have some brain left in me. So, why am I recommending the most "script kiddie" operating system here. Well, that's precisely why actually. When it all comes down to it, Ubuntu is easy. A beginner hacker doesn't need too many fancy tools or a Linux distribution geared for the precise 5 commands they use regularly. No, an aspiring hacker needs ease of use, they need an operating system that doesn't make them think about why they ever split away from Windows.

This kind of seamless integration of other OS users into Linux exists only with Ubuntu. Plus, it's not like it's horrible for hacking either. Obviously, it's not the pinnacle of hacking, and penetration testing tool development. On the other hand it does have a perfectly valid set of hacking tools available to it. Nothing that will make arch blush, mind you, but things that simply make it possible, which is all you really need as a beginner.

Now, as we've said before, we'll be using Kali Linux, so let's get you up to speed, shall we?

Kali Linux

Kali Linux is a platform used for security auditing and penetration testing. It uses advanced tools which makes it one of the best ways to detect and identify vulnerabilities that can possibly happen at the network environment that a programmer or a hacker targets. If you have objectives that are specific and defined, and if you apply testing methodology accordingly, you will get a robust penetration testing and accurate results.

Short History and the Purpose of Kali Linux

Kali Linux is often referred to as just Kali. It stands for a distribution system from Linux, and it was developed specifically for penetration testing purposes. The first name for this system was actually BackTrack, and it represented a kind of merger that was supposed to connect Auditor IWHAX and WHOPPIX penetration testing distributions. BackTrack gained enormous popularity, and with more than 4 million downloads all over the world represents one of the most popular distribution systems that Linux has ever made. The first version of Kali, however, was released in 2013. This version had issues with USB for the keyboard so it wasn't long before a new version was out on the market and it had that issues fixed. The success of Kali Linux was obvious after just five days because, in the period between these two first Kali versions (five days), the system was already downloaded around 100 000 times.

There are some major characteristics of Kali Linux that you should be aware of, and you can find more details about them on its official website.

First of all, you should know that Kali Linux is made using Debian Linux distribution and it has around 300 applications for penetration testing.

Kali Linux is excellent when it comes to wireless card support.

Its packet injection has a custom kernel patched to it, and all of its software packages have their developers sign them with a GPG.

Kali Linux supports systems that are based on ARM, and you can customize it to your own preferences.

As we mentioned, the main focus behind releasing Kali Linux is that it should be used for security auditing and for penetration testing. However, these are not simple tasks and there are a series of complex activities that have to be executed for Kali to achieve its purpose. For example, although it is a system, Kali was designed as a framework. The reason for this is that this system has various tools that cover all sorts of use cases. All of these tools can be used individually or in combination depending on the nature of the penetration test. Additionally, Kali Linux is not limited to just one kind of device. This system can be used on several computer types, such as laptops and system administrators' servers. It can be used for network monitoring, for analysis in forensic cases, and so on.

Furthermore, you can add Kali Linux to embedded stealthy devices like ARM which can be placed on a place with wireless networks or it can be simply plugged into the computer that you are targeting. ARM devices can be extremely useful, but they can also be attack machines that cause many problems. In both cases, the biggest advantage of an ARM is that it has a small number of form factors and that you don't need requirements of high power. That's not all, Kali Linux has another useful trait, it can be put on the cloud, and it can do a quick check on password cracking cases.

This system is not limited to one, but to all kinds of computers; it can be used for penetration testing for your phone or your tablet too. Nevertheless, penetration testers can't work without external servers, which is why Kali has a collaboration software that can be used by a group that does a test penetration. Kali uses this software to set up a server on the web and use it for running scanning tools for vulnerability, campaigns for phishing activities, and all other things related to it. When you install Kali, you will notice that the main menu of this system has a theme that organizes all activities.

Installation Specifics

The first step of using Kali Linux is to download it and install it. The safest way to get this system is to go directly to its website: http://www.kali.org/downloads/ and you shouldn't have any problems if you choose the official image of Kali on the download page. You should pay attention to the following items and make sure that you have the real version. The items you should be aware of are machine architecture and image type. When it comes to machine architecture, the specification should be i386, amd64, armel, and armhf. Additionally, image type should be either VMware image or ISO image, depending on your needs.

There are few differences between ISO and VMware images for you to consider before Kali installation. Firstly, if you use the ISO image version, you should know that it is a good option for burning images on DVDs for example. On the other hand, VMware is in a version that is used to analyze the virtual environment and then speed up configuration and installation. When you choose the image file and download it, the next step is to see the SHA1 values of the image that you downloaded and its value on the page.

Compare those values and try to confirm if the page has its integrity and true information. This method is also useful to prevent you from installing files that are not good and that contain viruses or some other malicious data. When it comes to the UNIX/Linux/BSD operating system, there are commands such as sha1sum that you can use to check if the hash value of your SHA1 downloaded image is right. If the process takes some time, it is ok because the hash value can be big, thus the system needs more time to process all of the data. Let's take an example, let's say that you want to determine the level of the hash value for the file: kali-Linux-1.0.1-i386.iso.

You would use the command like:

sha1sum kali-Linux-1.0.1-i386.iso
41e5050f8709e6cd6a7d1baaa3ee2e89f8dfae83 kali-Linux-1.0.1-i386.iso

If you have a Windows operating system, you can use many tools for SHA1 hash value. To generate it, there is a tool named sha1sum for instance. This tool can be found at http://www.ring.gr.jp/ pub/net/gnupg/binary/sha1sum.exe, and it is widely applied because it doesn't take much space and because it simply works for every computer model. Still, if you don't want to use sha1sum, there is, of course, and alternative to it. The easiest way to use one is to go to HashMyFiles. This tool supports algorithms such as SHA-512, SHA-256, CRC32,

MD5, obviously SHA1, and many more. The easiest way to apply HashMyFiles is to run it after you downloaded it, and use the navigation to select SHA1 hash value to the desired file. If you want a shortcut, you can press F2 and do the exact same thing and choose the image that you prefer.

When the SHA1 value appears on the Kali Linux download page you need to compare it with the hash value of the tools that you used to generate it (using sha1sum for example). You can start using Kali's next sections only if these two values match. However, if the value that is displayed and the value that you got don't match, you have an issue of broken file. The simplest way to resolve it is to download the image again. Remember, use the official website's sources because that is the safest way, and make sure that the hash values match in each case. There are multiple ways that you can use Kali Linux, some of them are:

- To run Kali using its official Live DVD

- To download and install Kali on the hard disk of your computer and then start using it

- Lastly, you can have portable Kali by installing it on your USB memory disk.

You need to be aware of the fact that each professional that uses Kali for security purposes has to do a verification process for their tools. The goal of authentication is to protect clients and their networks, along with all the data that Kali Linux will have access to. The first step is already in the downloading process. As a matter of fact, Kali's website uses TLS protection; however, the link for download doesn't have an encrypted URL which makes it vulnerable for some kinds of middle attacks. Take into consideration that Kali uses a large network of external mirrors.

The point is, that you need to be extra careful when you download the images that we mentioned above because some of these mirrors may be compromised at one point. It isn't likely, but it isn't impossible that you can end up as a victim of a cyber-attack. To prevent this, Kali Linux has set different image checksums, and to make its authentication more effective, this hash checksum has to be the same on the image that you have on your computer and the one set by developers.

A Detailed Tour of Kali

As we said, Kali Linux has numerous tools that can be used to achieve different goals. However, all of these goals are mostly connected to penetration testing. And since having that many tools without any organization would make Kali difficult to use, they were set into categories that we will view in the following part of this section.

The first category is called Information gathering. In this category, you can find tools that you can use to collect information about operating systems and networks. Also, you can use it to know more about DNS, IDS/IPS, SSL, VPN, and IP of voice over. Additionally, you can use it to gather information on e-mail addresses, SMB, SNMP, and VPN.

The second category in Kali Linux concerns assessments for vulnerability. Here you can find tools that will deal with vulnerability issues in general, but some tools will help you get to the Cisco network. Also, you can find a few fuzzing tools that can be useful to assess vulnerable servers.

The next category is also a widely used one, and it is known as web applications. As its name suggests, this category has tools that help you manage web applications using various methods. You can take app fuzzes, app proxies or vulnerability scanners.

You can exploit the web application content along with their full databases.

Password attacks are the next group of tools that we will mention. It has tools that will provide you with a successful attack on passwords whether you are offline or online.

The category of exploitation tools is also a big one. It has numerous ways to detect vulnerabilities in the network environments that you are targeting. The most commonly used tools from this category are tools for database, network and Web checks. Additionally, you can find tools that can be used for so-called social engineering attacks. Exploit tools can give you more insight into the kind of information that was exploited if such a thing happens.

The sixth category has an authentic name; it is known as sniffing and spoofing. In this category, you will find tools that you can use to really sniff the web traffic of the network environment that you are targeting, and the network itself. On the other hand, the most commonly used tools when it comes to spoofing are tools known as Yersinia or Ettercap.

There are also tools gathered into the category of access maintenance. They allow you to access the machine you are targeting and, as its name suggests, to maintain the access to that machine. Still, to install such tools into the specific machine might require you to have the highest permissions (like admin). There are also tunneling tools that can be found under this category, along with the tools for "backdooring".

In the category of reporting tools are all kinds of tools that are useful for results, processes, and other sorts of documentations that are connected to the penetration testing of the targeted environment.

Lastly, there are system services such as MySQL or Apache that provide you support during penetration testing. Additionally, you can use tools like Metasploit or SSH.

Kali Linux has its own Top 10 tools for security that were made having penetration testers in mind. The goal of this list was to make it easier for testers and create a kind of shortcut at least when it comes to the tool's choice. It is important to know that this list is made based on the frequency of use by the penetration testers. So, the top 10 tools for security at this point are aircrack-ng, burp-suite, hydra, john, maltego, Metasploit, Nmap, SQLmap, Wireshark, and ZAproxy.

Even though these are the top 10, there are few more groups divided by a purpose that we would like to point out.

The first group of tools is the one used for wireless attacks. You can use them to target all kinds of wireless devices, as their name suggests, along with the RFID/NFC and Bluetooth connections.

A second group is a group of tools used for reverse engineering. They can be used when you need to disassemble a file that can be executed or when there is a program that you need to debug.

A group of stress testing tools is useful for stressing the Web environment of your targeted network, along with its wireless and VOIP.

Another useful tool group is the one for hardware hacking. These tools can be used in applications that are made in Arduino or Android.

Forensics is a group of tools that are mostly used in digital processes. For example, you can use a tool from this group to carve files, to get an image of a hard disk or to analyze it. If you want a proper use of these capabilities in Kali, you must learn how to navigate to Kali Linux Forensics | No Drives. Alternatively, you can use the booting menu and do a Swap Mount. Whatever option you choose from these two, your drives won't be mounted automatically. In general, this means that your drive will keep their integrity since no one can connect automatically to them.

So, as you have had the opportunity to see, Kali Linux has numerous tools that are made for specific uses. Note that there is an option to set Kali Linux as the main operating system on a computer. Even though Kali has almost every characteristic that any Linux distribution does, there are few additional that it can be helpful to overview for those who are interested in penetration testing or security issues.

- One of the features that differ Kali from other Linux distributions is its Live System. This means that when you download ISO image from the official website, its only task isn't to install Kali as your operating system. It can have an additional use. This use reflects in becoming a bootable live system which means that there is a possibility of using Kali without actually installing it on your computer. You can achieve this by copying the ISO image on one of your USB keys and booting it.

- We have already mentioned the Forensics tool group, however, there is a Forensic mode too. When your computer is in this mode it means that there can't be any activities that could influence the data in any manner. This mode works on a simple principle- it is enabled using the boot menu and it will prevent any kind of activity that could auto-mount disc that the desktop could have detected. The forensic model is often used in combination with a live system that we viewed above because it allows you to reboot the system without hard disk modifications.

- There is a Custom Linux Kernel for Kali Linux that is designed using a Debian Unstable version as its basis. The purpose of this Kernel is to ensure that a system has good support for hardware, even more, when you are working with devices that use wireless. Kernels are usually patched to fit injection support for wireless. The reason is that there is a large number of tools for wireless security that rely exclusively on Kali's feature. Almost every hardware device needs firmware files that are up to date. These files are usually found on special libraries such as /lib/firmware/, but in Kali Linux, they are installed by default. Additionally, Kali installs even the firmware that is located in a non-free section of Debian.

- There is an option of completely customizable Kali. And its main trait is that it is built by penetration testers for those who are using it for the same purposes. However, since not everyone uses the same kind of tools, there is an option to customize the system by using tools that are more suitable for your preferences. To achieve this, Kali Linux developers have put a configuration that can be used for the live-building of Kali images (official ones) which enables you to make your own version of the system. If you choose to use this option, you will see that it is not difficult to make changes since there is a versatile choice of live-build options. You can install files with supplementary roles, modify the system, add packages or arbitrary commands, and so on.

- Another unique characteristic of Kali Linux is that it has a "Trustable Operating System. This means that users have the right to know if Kali can be trusted, and the best way to achieve that, according to Kali's developers, was to make this program and its improvements public. Anyone interested in Kali can find and go through the source code, thus determine if it can be trusted or not. The advantage of Kali is that it was made by developers who are knowledgeable and transparent, yet they used the best practices known today in terms of data security. So for example, they build daemons by using source packages that are signed directly by them, which provides a kind of guarantee that the code is trustworthy. Additional security check after that is that all these packages have to be check-summed before they can go to a signed repository where they should be further distributed on a full review using 14 repositories. These repositories are the basis of Kali's source packages and each package can be tracked by using the tracker15 command.

- A final unique trait of Kali that we will mention here is its ability to penetrate a wide range of ARM devices because it has a variety of binary packages. All these packages are used for architectures such as arm64, armel, and armhf ARM. And since Kali is easy to install, multiple interesting devices can be used for penetration, from tablets and smartphones to computers and Wi-Fi routers of all kinds.

Note that Kali's main target group is IT, administrators and security professionals. It is not a mainstream operating system but rather defined as a rolling distribution that has updates daily. The basis of Kali Linux is Debian Testing 18 so almost all packages that you can use in Kali can be found on the repository of Debian too. Although Kali's main definition is to enable security auditing and penetration testing it is not limited to only that. Kali can be used to monitor your network or wireless, to perform a different kind of analysis using forensic mode, and so forth. Also, Kali Linux has a user-friendly menu that enables you to choose tools for a wide range of tasks quickly and without major problems. Some of the tasks that can be executed by Kali's tools are password and wireless attacks, vulnerability, and web app analysis, reverse engineering, snooping, system services, etc. When it comes to the advanced features, Kali differs from other Linux distribution with its live systems, robust forensic mode, option for customization, ARM capability, and many other possibilities.

Basic Commands, Search, And Directories

Kali Linux has an enormous number of commands. You can find the simplest ones, such as getting date and time to the more complicated ones like commands for handling documents or finding and maintaining directories, etc. In the following section we will list some of the most frequently used, thus the basic commands that can be implemented in Kali Linux:

Getting the date is one of the simplest yet most frequently used commands in Kali. As its name suggests, you can use this command to see a date and time while using Kali Linux on your computer. If you want to set a certain date, you can do it by using the # date –set= command for example.

Let's say you want the 17th of September, that would look like: #date-set='10 Sept 2019 17:16'The output of this command displaying on your screen will be Tue Sept 10 17:16 EDT 2019

Another command that is simple yet used a lot, is a command for the calendar. This is one of the key commands of Kali, and if you use it, it will start a calendar that is already built into the

Linux terminal screen. Nevertheless, Kali Linux has additional packages that allow you to handle the calendar in different ways. If you want to download this additional package, you have to go to the official website, find a package named call, and add it to your local machine that uses Linux operational system.

The commands, Whoami and who, are very popular and useful. The first one gives you username and info about who executes a certain command while the other is used when you want to view the entire information (all details) about the person logged in into the system.

PWD is short for Print Working Directory. This command is used in Kali Linux when you want to display a certain directory. This command will also display the one who is the owner of the command executed at the time. You may lose track of the directory you got into so you can use this command and view the information you need.

Another frequently used command in Kali Linux is simply Ls. When you understand the logic behind this command, it can rapidly become the first command that you use when accessing Kali. In general, Ls is used to get you the full list of documents that are stored in the needed directory. This command has additional extended commands and they are mostly used to show these lists properly (to avoid chaos). For example, if you use Ls-lrt or Ls-al, you will get more information about lists that are about to be displayed from the wanted directory.

Cd is a Kali Linux command that you can use to alter the directory that is already on Kali's platform. On the other hand, you can use Mkdir if you want to create your own directory.

Cat is also a commonly used and if you execute it, it will show you the full content of a specific file. There is an additional use of this command since you can create one or more files directly in Kali's platform. Cp is a command that is used to copy the images of the files that are already in directories. By using this command you can paste that same file anywhere you want in Kali, and you can even put it under a different name.

There are commands that you can use for displaying and modifying text files. If you use the cat-file command to concatenate files it will display its content on the Linux terminal. If the size of the file is too big, there is an option of using pager and displays the file page by page. Then you can use editor command and edit the targeted text. This command enables you to modify and create a text file. If the file is simple, you can create it directly if you execute the following: command >file. However, if you use command >>file the file will be appended rather than overwriting it.

Kali Linux can be a little frustrating until you become familiar with it, and sometimes it can be hard to find your way around. However, there are a few commands that you can use to make it easier to work in this system at first. The fundamental command for this aspect is a searching command that is called simply "locate". This is also one of the easiest ones. You usually use "locate" with a certain keyword that will go through the entire system and find every file and location that corresponds to the given keyword.

Let's say you want to find "example"; you can use the following:

kali >locateexample-ng /usr/bin/example

/usr/share/applications/kali-example.desktop
/usr/share/desktop-directories/05-1-01-example.directory

 --snip-- /var/lib/dpkg/info/example.mg5sums

Chapter 3: An Introduction to Scripting

Now then, how do you start scripting? Well, the first, and easiest thing you'll need is a text editor. You'll need one that's...well...capable of processing text? That's really all you need to begin.

Starting Bash is quite straightforward, you just have to start typing "bash" directly into the prompt of the shell. However, this will only work assuming that one of the variables (PATH variable) is set accurately. Another important thing that you should know about installing Bash is that even if you are not the "root user" on your computer and you don't have all of the privileges that come with it, it is still possible to install and use Bash if you have your own account. If this is the case you will have to specify another directory for installing bash rather than the one we mentioned above. Also, you will have to use the prefix option to make sure that you configured the location of Bash correctly. For instance, you can install it on your "home" page which means that you configure that with the following code: —prefix=$HOME or — prefix=$HOME/.

Open up your text editor of choice and type in the following:

#!/bin/bash

Script Number 1

echo "Script Number 1 is number 1!"

This will, when run, output " Script Number 1 is number 1!" Without the quotation marks. And there you go! Now, you might ask what every one of these lines means, and I'll be happy to answer.

So, first off "#!/bin/bash" is called the shebang. The shebang is always the first line of the script (yes, even if the 1st line is blank, you can't have the shebang 2nd.) Now, "#!" is the part of the line referred to as the shebang itself, if we're being pedantic. The rest of it is the path that the interpreter should use in order to interpret the rest of the script. For Bash scripts you don't need to learn much of this, as the path will almost always be to Bash.

#Script Number 1 is a comment. It doesn't do anything, however, it serves as a kind of note within the code which can help you know what you were doing, and where you got to.

Echo is the first command you're getting to. It means "output this string on the screen." A string is just a fancy word for a set of letters and symbols, so whatever you put after the echo command, the script will "say."

Now, it's worth noting that a deeper introduction to Bash awaits you in the second book of this series, however, let's go into it just a little bit more with variables.

You've probably already encountered variables in your life before. In math problems, those would be the "X's" and "Y's" of the world. They refer to values that we are not certain about, however, we can either deduce, or assign their values.

Let's look at an example, shall we?

#!/bin/bash

Here, we set one variable to be equal to Hello, and the other one to Goodbye

firstvar =Hello

secondvar=Goodbye

echo $firstvar$secondvar

Echo

In this scenario, the output you'll be facing on the screen will be "Hello Goodbye" this is because we've referred to it under $firstvar and $secondvar. When declaring a variable (telling the script it exists) we do not write the $ sign. However, when referring to it later on in the script, it is necessary. Keep in mind that when you write your code.

Variables are extremely useful, and are the backbone of every scripting language. Now let's take a look at how to interact with them using the read method:

```
#!/bin/bash
```

Here you'll be inputting a string value for the variable to be equal to.

echo Hello, what is the meaning of life, fellow human being?

#varname is the variable you'll be setting

read varname

echo

Ah, so the meaning of life, my fellow human being, is indeed $varname ? That is truly fascinating. I'll be sure to tell the brood.

While this ominous piece of text might be a testament to the fact that I get carried away writing these examples sometimes, it also shows how easy it is to manipulate the value of a variable. While naming it "read" might not have been the most intuitive of the Bash developers (it's almost as if they considered the computer more of a person than the programmer.) It's still extremely simple. The only thing you need to remember is that if you decide to refer to the variable later, it needs to be with a $ sign behind it.

Bash can be defined as a standard shell that comes with almost every Linux distribution, but we can't say that it is the only one. In fact, no rule says how Bash has to be present in any specific distribution. However, it is still one of the most widely used shells for scripting in Linux. There is another way to view Bash, it can be seen as a software that is open-sourced and released under GPL (short for GNU Public Licence). So, to use Bash, obviously, you first have to make sure that you have it on your computer. If don't, you can download it from http://www.gnu.org (FSF or Free Software Foundation), or you can simply use one of its mirrors. Note that Bash installation comes in source code of C programming language and that its installation procedure can be different from time to time. In most cases, the installation process is automated. We will give you some basic pointers that you will probably encounter during installation, but if you want complete instructions, you should read files that come with the source code when you initially download Bash.

Firstly, you need to check your configuration and see the version of your operating system. You can use a configure program to check this. Without proper specification, you won't know if your operating system has all features that are needed for Bash to work.

The next step is to run '' make". This step will build Bash on your computer.

After you've run '' make", the next thing you need to do is to run '' make tests". This step is important because it will start the diagnostic. Without it, you can't be sure if Bash is built properly in the first place.

Only after you've done all this, in most of the cases, you will have the option to run " make install". When you hit this run, Bash will stay in your computer in some of the local directories. Most often you will find it in the /usr/local/ subdirectory, which is, as its name suggests, a local subdirectory of your computer.

There are scripting languages that are similar to Bash, but they are not identical to it. Some of the most commonly used ones are Python, Perl and Korn shell better known as Ksh. The last one (Korn shell), for example, represents an upgraded version of previously used Bourne shell and it even has its version for a public domain which is known as "pdksh". UNIX systems use Ksh most of the time which is why this shell has its own audience and popularity.

On the other hand, Ksh's features work under the Bash shell although there are few exceptions; for example, both Bash and Ksh can perform bitwise arithmetic operations. Both shells may have the same features but that they are named differently. For instance, Ksh has a "print" command that is built in the shell, and we can say that this "print" command is more or less equivalent to the "printf" command that we have in Bash. Another example can be Bash's "type" command that has a pretty much the same function as Ksh's command "whence".

If you are interested in knowing all differences that can be found between Bash shell and other shells, you can go to http://www.faqs.org/faqs/unixfaq/shell/bash/, which is actually the Bash's FAQ and find all this information.

Another scripting language that has its similarities with Bash is Practical Extraction and Report Language, otherwise known as simply Perl. Perl's main purpose, as its name says, is to generate reports. The most distinctive feature of Perl is that it uses a combination of features and commands that allow it to build a tool necessary for the completion of a single task. In most cases, the tool combination contains some shell language features along with commands like "sed" and "awk". Keep in mind that even though Perl uses some traits of shell scripting, it is not compatible with Bash shell.

Lastly, we have Python, which has some similar characteristics with Bash. To recap, Python got its name after the British comedy group "Monty Python" and it represents an interpreted language used for projects that are small but need fast and effective development. Remember that both Bash and Python have interactive session features, however, scripts made in Python are never compatible with scripts made in Bash.

Keywords and Command Basics In Bash

Like all languages, Bash has its own set of keywords and commands that are used for navigating through and scripting in Bash. First of all, we will explain what a keyword is. In both scripting and programming languages, keywords are usually symbols or words that have a particular meaning in the language of your computer. In the following section, we will give you both- words and symbols that are used, Bash. Keep in mind that they function as a keyword when they are the first word in the command and unquoted. They are as follows:

!   esac   select   }   case   fi   then
[[do

for		until	]]		done		function
while	elif						

if		time	else	in		{

Most of the languages don't allow that their keywords are used as names of the variables. Still, Bash has that option regardless of the fact that it can be a cause of creating almost unreadable scripts. Note that even if Bash offers such an option, you should avoid using keywords in this manner. As we explained, if the keyword is the name of the variable at the same time, you will have a hard time working with it, but if you keep the names of the variables and keywords separately, you will get scripts that are far more understandable, thus easier to use.

On the other hand, we have Bash shell's commands. These commands are stored externally to the file system using a Linux program. Commands used in Bash are mostly the ones that can be typed at the shell prompt, but some of them are already built in the shell. Mostly these types of built-in commands are connected to the standardization of the language, its speed or if that is the only way for the program to function without any major issues. Regardless of the type of the source they come from, commands are still considered as informal categories of the language, and Bash is no exception.

We have commands for the general-purpose called utilities that are used in countless applications. Some of these commands are date return or calculating how many lines of code are in the targeted file.

Another type of command frequently used is called filters. These commands are used to use results from other commands, modify them (for example, it replaces words or removes the code lines that are not wanted), and then forward them further. If the circumstances are right, a large number of commands can be used as filters. The fastest way to execute any command in Bash is to type it at its command prompt.

Note that in Bash, this prompt is usually represented with symbol $, but it happens often that Linux customizes this symbol into something else. For instance, certain programs use > as the command prompt instead of $.

For example, if you type a date command, you will have the time and date currently set on your computer. In Bash, that would look like this:

$ date Wed Oct 1 11:44:52 EDT 2019

Please keep in mind that all commands and files in any programming or scripting language are case sensitive. By convention, it is determined that all commands that are used in shells for scripting, have to be written in lowercases.

If you write something like this:

$ DATE bash: DATE: command not found

You will need an argument. If you have an argument, it means that you will have some additional information that will supply a command you want and influence it to change the way it behaves. If we stick to the date command, one of the arguments is a "format" because it influences the way date and time will appear on the screen. For instance, you can write an argument like this:

$ date '+%H:%M' 11:44

Another command that you should be aware of is a switch. Two other names are used for this command so you can find it like an option or a flag. Switches are usually characters used to enable a certain feature. They are usually executed by using a sign "-". For example, if you want to display the date in UTC (Coordinated Universal Time is previously known as GMT) you will use the following switch command: "-u". In code, that looks like this:

$ date -u Wed Oct 11 14:46:41 UTC 2019

The reason why we call this command a switch rather than a flag or option is the fact that the other two words have wide usage in various contexts. So the main reason is to avoid confusion.

We mentioned both arguments and switches and their meaning, however, in the context of programming, these two terms are referred to as parameters. The reason why we point this out is that there are commands that use these parameters and make complex combinations of them all the time.

Also, when it comes to switches, according to the convention between Linux and GNU, if you want to have a more readable command, you use double "−" instead of one, this means that −u has its longer (more readable) equivalent which is -- universal. In code, that looks like this:

$ date --universal Wed Oct 11 14:46:41 UTC 2019

Longer switches are useful because they remind those who are reading the code, what the switch exactly does. This kind of feature is especially significant for shell debugging because it makes it easier. Unfortunately, debugging doesn't have a standardized convention like commands when it comes to short switches in Linux. Most frequently, Linux will only recognize and react only on the switches that are long, such as " -- version", or "--help". In Bash, you can add comments at the end of a certain command, or you can just type them to stand alone in the line. Still, make sure that you put denotation sign # in front of every comment. We will stick with the date code as an example, and with the comment added to it, the code will now look like this:

$ date --universal # show the date in UTC format

As we mentioned, some commands are already built into Bash, such as "- -a" which is treated as a special switch. If you see this switch it means that the action has to be executed only after all other switches are done. Additional use of this switch is to combine it with one argument by using a single "-" sign.

In Bash, there exists a combination of special keys that allow you to edit commands that you previously typed in, or to repeat them if needed. It is useful to know that Bash has two modes for editing and that they emulate two text editor keys that are popularly used in Linux. The first mode is the "Vi" mode and it imitates "vi" and "vim" text editors from Linux. The second mode is "emacs" mode that mimics Linux text editors known as "emacs", "pico" or "nano". If you want to check the editing mode you are using at the moment, you can do that by executing a command named "shopt". If you are in "emacs" mode you will see "shopt-o emacs" which means literally that mode is on. Contrarily, if you see "shopt-o vi" it means that this mode is on, therefore you are working in "vi" editing mode. Note that in Bash only one mode can be active at a time, which means that you can't use both modes at the same time. In code, "on" and "off" of these modes can be written like this:

$ shopt -o emacs emacs on

$ shopt -o vi off

On the other hand, we have arrow keys that work as a cursor regardless of the editing mode you are in. The arrows go through the commands that are most recently executed selecting the ones you are interested in. The function of each arrow is as following:

- The up arrow will take you to the previously executed command when you go through command history.

- The down arrow will move you to the command executed next if there is any after the one you are at.

- The right arrow will always move your position one character to the right side in the command history

- The left arrow, on the contrary, will move you one character back to the left side. Note that arrows don't delete characters, they just move through them.

Now, since "emacs" mode is the mode that is on by default on almost every Linux distribution (which means Bash has this default mode too), you should know how these same commands function in "emacs" keys:

In "emacs" mode, control-b has the function of the left arrow which means that it moves you one character to the left without erasing anything. The next command function is control-f that has the same function as the right arrow (moving you one character to the right side as we mentioned above). The third command is control-p that has the same function as up arrow, leading you to the command that was previously used in the program while control-n command moves you forward if there are some commands after the one you are currently at.

The additional command that we didn't explain before, thus it doesn't have equivalent like the others, is the tab key. When you press the tab key you will execute the command of finding filenames that match, if there are any. This is actually an act of filename completion and its purpose is to match the file name with the final word that appears on the code line. If there is a match, the rest of the name is automatically typed in Bash. If we take date command as an example again, we will see that $ dat is done when you press the Tab key to it.

If you are in the ''vi' mode, the commands and their functions differ. So here are the basic ones:

You will use Esc- command if you want to exit or enter the mode for editing. If you want to move to the left without erasing characters (like a left arrow), in ''vi'' mode you will use h- command. Also, if you want to move right for one character (like a right arrow), in this mode you will use l- command. If you want to move back (equivalent to up arrow), you will use k- command, and if use j- command it will lead you to the next executed command in history if there is any. Additionally, if you press Esc two times while in ''vi'' mode, you will get the same outcome as if you press Tab in the previous "emacs" mode.

The full list of combinations that can be used in Bash is beyond the scope of this book, but you can find it on the main page of Bash (also known as the reading line section). Although some key combinations are set by default, they are not fixed. You can adjust them if you use commands like ''bind''. At first, the best choice is to use default combinations, and if you have some specific project in mind, you can take your time and see which of these default combination can be the best solution for customization. All keys beside the default ones are controlled by the set teletype command (stty) from old Linux. If you execute this command you will have insight into all keys that are commonly used as command keys, and all sorts of information that can be useful for your session. If you want to switch these settings, you can use a switch (remember what we mentioned before about switches). If you wish to change complete settings you can use −a (switch for all), and the code will be as follows:

$ stty speed 9600 baud; evenp hupcl

intr = ^C; erase = ^?; kill = ^X;

eol2 = ^@; swtch = ^@;

susp = ^Z; dsusp = ^Y;

werase = ^W;

lnext = ^@;

-inpck -istrip icrnl -ixany ixoff onlcr

-iexten echo echoe echok

-echoctl −echoke

Note that most of the settings we have talked about here are used when you work with serial port devices. If that is not the case, you can even ignore them. On the other hand, some settings are used to control the combination of keys marked with the" ^" symbol. Keep in mind that there is no definition for keys that use " ^@" marks. Here are some basic meanings of key combination settings:

- Erase, which is presented with ^? Moves you left while erasing one character with each move.

- Intr, which is presented with ^C stops or interrupts the line of the program you are currently in.

- Kill, presented with ^X is used to erase the line you are currently on

- Reprint, presented with ^R is usually used to redraw the line you are currently targeting

- Stop, otherwise written as ^S is used to pause the program and allows you to read the results of your current work.

- Start, written as ^Q and used to resume the program that you paused before.

- Werase, written as ^W is used to delete the word that you typed last in the program.

Bash has a command history that contains all commands that are executed recently. You can see it as a list and the easiest way to browse it and find the command you are looking for is to use arrow keys (up and down). If you want an alternative way, you can use ! or exclamation mark to perform the same action. This mark is used to denote the command that has to be executed next and completed using Bash. Keep in mind that Bash will always execute the commands that match and are recent. Sticking with the date example, the code for this action would be as follows:

$ date

Wed Oct 11 11:55:58 EDT 2019

$!d

Wed Oct 11 11:55:58 EDT 2019

If Bash doesn't find a command that matches, you will get feedback like this:

$!x

bash: !x: event not found

If you want to repeat the command that you last gave to Bash, you just have to use a double exclamation mark. In that case, the code will be like this:

$ date

Thu Oct 11 14:03:25 EDT 2019

$!! date

Thu Oct 11 14:03:28 EDT 2019

The advantage of the exclamation mark (!) command is that it can be used in various situations, and it can even create a shortcut if the circumstances are right. For example, if you have a negative number in the line code, it indicates that you have a relative number of lines. Generally speaking, this means that the negative number will command how many commands you have to go back to find the one to execute, so if you write !! or !-1 it will give you the same result. In code, that will look like this:

$ date

Thu Oct 11 14:04:54 EDT 2019

$ printf "%s\n" $PWD

/home/kburtch/

$!-2 date

Thu Oct 11 14:05:15 EDT 2019

The additional command that you can add to repeat the content of the line we have just written is !#. Note that this is not the same as #! that you use in shell scripts; the repeat command, in this case, is used to run a specific set of commands two times. Again, in the code line, that looks like this:

$ date ; sleeps6 ; !#

date ; sleep 6 ; date ; sleep 6 ;

Fri Oct 18 17:26:54 EST 2019

 Fri Oct 18 17:26:59 EST 2019

If you look for a file that contains command history, Bash keeps it under name .bash_history. The only situation in which this is not the case is when you define a variable called HISTFILE. If you cancel a Bach session, all the commands that you used during that session will be saved in the history file we just mentioned. And every time you start a new session in Bach, you can access all commands that you used in previous sessions (until the maximum data size is completed).

Bash offers another option known as '' hisverify" that allows you to alter commands that you retrieved, which means that they are not executed automatically like in other cases. In Bash, you can have full control over the complete command history thanks to its built-in commands. You can specify the number of lines you want to see and avoid listing the whole history. Again, the code for doing this is, for example:

$ history 11

1026 set -o emacs

 1027 stty

1028 man stty

1029 stty -a

1030 date edhhh

1031 date edhhh

1032 date

1033 date

1034 !

1035 history 11

If you want to delete an entry from history, you can use −d command. Then the code will be:

$ history −d

1029 $ history 11

1027 stty

1028 man stty

1029 date edhhh

1030 date edhhh

1031 date

1032 date

1033 !

1034 history 11

1035 history -d 1029

Commands for Directories In Bash

Bash has also built-in directories. One of them is a present working directory, and if you use –in pwd command it will execute the return of the current directory's name in Bash. For example:

$ pwd

 /home/kburtch

Even though this is a simple command, the present working directory has a few switches that can be used. Some of them are:

P, a physical switch used to show the real directory.

-L is a logical switch used to show symbolic links of the directories.

For instance, if you have a link to a directory /user_drive/homes, and that link is if /home, these switches will work in the code like this:

pwd -P

/user_drive/homes/kburtch

 $ pwd -L /home/kburtch

Bash offers another built-in command known as change directory (-cd) that, as its name suggests, changes the one you are currently in. Again, in code, this command is executed as follows:

pwd

/home/kburtch

```
$ cd .

$ pwd
/home/kburtch

$ cd ..

$ pwd /home

$ cd kburtch

$ pwd
/home/kburtch
```

Note that every time you use change directory command, the PWD variable is updated in Bash too. This variable is important because it has all the steps that will lead you again to the working directory you are currently working in.

Additionally, there is another variable that Bash maintains at all times, and you can find it under the name of OLDPWD. This variable doesn't have the current but the last directory you were working in. If you use the −cd command you can make a switch between directories (the previous one and the current one) which is an important shortcut that saves you a lot of time when you work in more than one directory. In code, this shortcut looks like this:

```
$ pwd

/home/kburtch

$ cd ..

$ pwd
```

/home

```
$ cd –
```

```
$ pwd
```

/home/kburtch

```
$ cd –
```

```
$ pwd
```

/home

You can add more than two directories and use the same principle.

This was the basic information that will allow you to do basic scripting in Bash. If you're looking to further your Bash knowledge, make sure to check out the sequel

Chapter 4: The Particulars Of Cybersecurity

Cybersecurity is considered to be a complex subject. There are numerous definitions, but as one of the most relevant ones, we will use the definition of NICCS or National Initiative for Cyber Security Careers and Studies. This definition says that Cybersecurity is: "The activity or process, ability or capability, or state whereby information and communications systems and the information contained therein are protected from and/or defended against damage, unauthorized use or modification, or exploitation."

This chapter will be used to explain some of the cybersecurity characteristics, and to explore why it's significant to know more about its connection with the economy, technology, and society in general. The fact is that technology and the services it offers are growing fast, and cyberspace becomes more and more incorporated in our daily lives. This is why policymakers along with other participants in all aspects of cybersecurity have to follow this growth, and constantly offer new solutions that will ensure growth and stability. Cyberspace is accessible to everyone which is why everyone must work together, to address challenges and find a way to resolve them.

The government of each country holds responsibility for developing strategies and policies concerning cybersecurity. On the other hand, the industry is considered to be the source of technology development and the implementation of these strategies. It is important to have people with operational experience and most of all, each country should make sure that they have the most significant components for this critical infrastructure. This kind of cooperation among multiple organizations and institutions has to find a common context. Also, you must be aware of the fact that industry not only develops and operates a big part of cyberspace but also owns it. The importance of a shared context is visible through regulatory policies that have to be consistent with the information flow. Cybersecurity is then achieved by adopting principles that are based on particular norms and of course best practices at the time.

Guidelines and Principles

In recent years, there have been numerous guides with all sorts of principles concerning the integration of technological, political, and societal aspects. In this chapter, we will mention principles that can be found at OECD guidelines for cybersecurity.

The first principle is awareness. It says that every participant in cyberspace has to be aware that network security is needed. Also, we all should be aware of the things we can do to improve that security because our personal information is often on the network too.

The second principle concerns responsibility. It says that every participant of the cyberspace holds a certain responsibility for its security and safety. The third is a response, and it points out that everyone should cooperate to prevent any kind of security incidents. Also, the goal is to work together to detect and provide necessary responses to these kinds of events too. The fourth principle in this guide talks about ethics and says that everyone should respect others and their interests as long as they are legitimate.

Also, the fifth principle points out that networks and system information and their security has to be correspondent with the most important values in societies with a democratic system. On the other hand, the sixth principle says that everyone in cyberspace should do risk assessments to prevent any inconveniences. The seventh principle talks about the implementation of particular security designs and how essential it is to incorporate such things into every information system.

It is said in the eighth principle that one of the tasks that all participants on networks should be aware of is to try to comprehend the importance and goals of security management in cyberspace. The last principle talks about the reassessment of the network. It says that everyone in cyberspace should make sure to participate in the modification of measures, practices, and procedures to improve the overall cybersecurity.

Norms are necessary for determining any kind of standardization. We can simply define norms as models or patterns that need to be followed. And they have to be correspondent with the technology in this case. Norms for cybersecurity follow principles that are also considered to be basic truths. This means that principles, in fact, represent a basis.

In this section, we will mostly talk about policies and their principles because they have the highest level of generalization. In this context, technical norms, for example, can be observed mostly by participants that have knowledge that is specialized for a certain area. We can say that there is no real physical border between principles and norms, or between technology and policy. And since the differences are not big, the consensus between all these areas is simpler to achieve. However, implementation can be a different matter since everything has to be taken into consideration.

One of the constructive approaches is finding policy principles between different areas and ensuring that technical norms, above all, are implemented and developed using these principles. One of the positive impacts of this kind of strategy would be finding industry norms that everyone can agree on. The concrete example of this type of consensus is the World Semiconductor Council that developed encrypting principles concerning one complicating area at the time.

Still, many things have to be taken into consideration to meet the requirements of the general incorporation of high-level principles. There are still many constraints, especially in policy designs, and the technology follows. Also, certain limitations influence the complexity of this type of environment. The main one is the slow response of policy change since it is not common to have technology experts making policies or policy experts making technological improvements. The main goal that cybersecurity has to nurture is to develop mechanisms that will transit principles into norms in the most objective way possible.

An example of a shared principle in cybersecurity strategies is support for privacy. However, the technical standards of each strategy and implementation of best practices are not necessarily the same. They can have different technology contexts and if they are not clear enough, it can lead to poor regulation that later influences internalization.

We can say that cybersecurity can't be achieved if there is no predictable way of connecting all of the best standards and norms. For instance, cybersecurity should have techniques that could make user anonymous, or recognize if someone is using that technique or for example, it should obtain a technique of obfuscating identifiers with unique traits.

We will give another example that represents technological constraints. For example, until now, technology couldn't provide 100% anonymity on the network. On the other hand, this feature is necessary if we want to create regulations that would protect data whether they are online or offline, as long as they are stored somewhere in cyberspace.

There is an ontology used by science that says how the connection of principles from policymakers and best practices from technology could be improved and designed in a manner of obtaining self-regulation at one point. Also, industry norms would have a bigger trust if predictability of potential attack would be more accurate. However, these multi-disciplinary consensuses are very complex and they need a lot of tools that would play a supportive role along with generally adopted norms and principles that will make a strong foundation.

More About Ontology

We already mentioned the ontology above. In computer science, ontology refers to giving formal names or defining properties of different types of entities in this case cyberspace. It is also used to describe relationships between different elements.

Ontology is useful in computer science because it enables you to point out the connections between different types of terms. It also helps you identify constraints and that is why it is frequently used in cybersecurity. Different kinds of ontology are used to create various settings in this area. For instance, they are often incorporated in models for developing systems that help against vulnerability. Ontology is useful to create organized and structured knowledge in various contexts.

The complexity of cybersecurity is described with ontology as a tool to connect the desired policy principles, best practices, and simplest technical norms. Ontology is used to explain the relationship between these concepts and ensures the design of accurate models when it comes to simulation of complex attacks and constraints that a certain system has.

An ontology that is well-created can be very significant when it comes to the framework for cybersecurity efficiency improvements. The benefits of this kind of framework would have multiple advantages and would improve the way of seeing technology space and its complexity by policymakers, and the design of norms and their correct context by industry.

Here are some ontology prepositions that are used as pointers in cybersecurity strategies' foundation:

The top layer or policy principles of the highest level can be built from concepts that are commonly accepted from before. On the other hand, technological characteristics can be described by adopting inputs from its environment with an experimental framework that can be used for analysis. And lastly, when developing and defining standards, norms, and best practices that are going to be incorporated into cybersecurity strategies, it should be done by including experts from different communities.

An ontology that can result by following these initiatives can lead to better results because it relies on background knowledge and addresses key issues that are accurate on more levels. This kind of ontology can empower more initiatives in multidisciplinary environments and enable more in-depth analysis, thus cybersecurity strategy improvements.

A good example of ontology implementation is CPS (Cyber-Physical Systems). It was developed because NIST11 proposed a framework that was risk-based and made CPS that links areas of safety, privacy, reliability, resilience, security, and all of that in a single, integrated model. The result of this kind of system was later used for creating standardization and regulation for IoT or Internet of Things. This integrated model is a classic presentation of general principles that are grouped into one set. This set can further be used to make proper analysis for the Internet of Things or IoT. This framework is used as a reference framework and it produced concrete elements that are later used to create pointers for making IoT systems in the future even more secure.

We can conclude that the main purpose of ontology in cybersecurity is to link principles that are under the high-level risk and to point out technical norms that can be used to improve their security. This kind of link allows technologists to develop more optimal technology along with the regulators who need to adjust the implementation strategies that govern this technical optimization.

Cybersecurity and the Technological Environment

When it comes to the technology environment, the main characteristic that affects cybersecurity is its dynamic evolution.

In the following paragraphs, we will describe some key characteristics of the technological environment that can be influential in cybersecurity. However, keep in mind that there are only the characteristics that are most commonly recognized ones, and they are broadly applicable rather than being specific. This categorization is based on attributes that are incorporated into foundations that we mentioned when we talked about ontology. We have two main categories: technological and societal. Technological further has sub-categorization into universal connectivity, dynamic nature, and complexity of technology, how technology influences our environment in a physical sense and technological infrastructure that has a shared nature. On the other hand, the societal category is further divided into the use of cyberspace that can be global and universal, and the impact of cyberspace that mostly refers to the economic aspect.

The main characteristics of the modern environment in computer science are known as ubiquitous connectivity and interoperability. They both refer to relationships between different devices, their systems, and ultimately, their networks. It is impossible to calculate the accurate amount of connected devices, but it is known that a number is very large.

Some estimations say that there are 7 billion people on the planet, and approximately 30 billion internet-connected devices will be used by the end of 2020. Others have predictions with even bigger numbers of devices connected by the internet; this amount goes up to 50 billion by the end of the next year. Take into consideration that many network domains that were separated ten or fifteen years ago are now merged. This way they support many different models and all sorts of connectivity providing them with network access. This access is granted because they all use shared cyberspace infrastructure.

There is a huge number of different devices connected through the internet that it would be almost impossible to count them all down. Some of these devices include PCs, tablets, data centers, disposable sensors, industrial control systems and so forth. All of these devices are matched using single criteria-network diversity. We mentioned ubiquitous connectivity before. This connectivity is especially useful for the economy because it has increased productivity and it is efficient at the same time. Also, it represents a platform in which all kinds of innovations are spread.

Although this kind of environment creates many challenges, most of them are known. On the other hand, universal connectivity and interoperability make threat analysis more complicated. It is harder to inspect the vulnerability of interconnected systems and establish whit kind of attacks can be expected and anticipated. Connectivity with its universal traits and interoperability with its broad application are the main factors in data movement, thus incredibly important for network policies standardization, and for networks and their security. Data localization is one of the aspects that define the internet as a network connection with an opened nature and there can be serious cybersecurity issues if this nature isn't anticipated and protected properly.

The foundation of the modern technology environment is based on interoperable networks. These networks usually have vulnerabilities that are not known immediately and the reason for that lays in the diversification of security models and their composition. There still haven't been developed any mechanisms that would completely analyze the complete internet infrastructure, even though it represents our reality today. The complexity of this process is obvious, and processing several domains at the same time is a typical thing for today's technological progress. Also, many technical domains may work to make just one operation successful. Even though there can be a single goal, different stages of interoperable networks have different kinds of vulnerabilities.

So it is very difficult to define so-called "trust evidence" in that kind of environment. There are no objective approaches that can estimate the security of a system when it has its operational conditions, especially if it is that complex.

Additionally, there are no common standards that can be applied in environments since they are not homogenized, and in which interoperable networks operate. And that is one of the main reasons why it is not that easy to predict the consequences that might happen when the system passes through many levels of environmental change. This refers to data protection also, not only to the environment. If the goal is to make an effective cybersecurity policy, policymakers have to fully understand all processes that happen in cyberspace and have enough examination to avoid oversimplification that can't follow the evolution capabilities of interoperable networks. Keep in mind that cybersecurity policies have to be neutral too so they can be incorporated correctly.

There is another characteristic important for linking the physical environment and cyberspace. We already mentioned CPS or Cyber-Physical Systems as an example. This is a system that has communication capabilities, computing components and finally, physical subsystems. Still, to be more effective, CPS has to develop cybersecurity models that are more complex and even more integrated than before. The unique trait of CPS is that it has intertwined domains like safety, reliability, privacy, and security even though traditionally, they should be separated.

The reason why CPS avoided using the traditional approach is the fact that separated domains can't properly address all possible risks. Also, the traditional approach neglected to see that the requirements of one domain can be used to access the risk composure of another domain if optimized properly. Also, unlike traditional systems, CPS has physical subsystems. The value of these components is connected to real-time controls that CPS has. It offers a different perspective on privacy and security requirements, and one of the examples is that CPS developed risk models even for the management of nuclear power stations.

As you may assume, in this kind of technical environment and network complexity safety and reliability are much more important than any other criteria. This means that security is not a top priority. This also means that when an attack happens, as it happened with Stuxnet (cyber-attack using a cyber-physical environment) CPS team realized that regardless of the crucial requirements, all kinds of risks have to be analyzed, anticipated and confronted.

Open Standards are important for sharing global infrastructure. The benefits of both are straightforward and clear to everyone. That means that we have the opportunity to use the same networks, devices, and processes all over the world, whether we live in Japan, or the USA or Egypt. As you know, technology is mostly based on one common language. It was important to reach a consensus in which all governments would allow sharing infrastructure so we have open standards that make a premise of the commercial internet. Still, there are always concerns about the dependability of this kind of global usage and many types of research from the beginning of the 90s have been focused on the protection of infrastructure.

Some approaches were working towards the militarization of cybersecurity, but many others focused on making cyberspace a safe place for education, transport, and many other functionalities that are necessary for people all around the globe. However, not all users have even expertise availability which is why different levels of cybersecurity appeared. This was also one of the main reasons why many people stressed the improvement of capacity building that will make cybersecurity stronger.

Statistic says that approximately 40% of the world had the internet in 2014. If you compare this information with connectivity percent in 1995, you will see that a difference is around 39%. The speed of technological evolution and network growth has unimaginable speed and it grows seven times faster than population numbers.

It is not surprising that such amount of users in cyber-space has an enormous influence on daily life. That is one more reason why it is required to examine the scope of cyberspace and its impact along with the frameworks that make it useful. Also, that is why one of the priorities is to have norms and practices that are broadly applicable and actionable in this kind of context. Sectors that are dealing with this particular matter influence the global economy. Here is another data: in 2010, 6% of global GDP was used for employment of the ICT sector. On the other hand, economic theories for cybersecurity develop slowly in comparison with technology development. That is why it is not uncommon to have issues in harmonization and implementation of policies made by using these theories.

Strategies for Cybersecurity

Every country has its own concepts of cybersecurity strategies. However, some organizations have global significance and their recommendations and analysis are considered to be relevant on a global level. Many of these organizations came to the same conclusion- every country shares some common elements when making cybersecurity strategies. These elements include approaches such as enhanced internal coordination of operations, the ability to create and rely on partnerships between public sectors and private sectors. Furthermore, they all imply that fundamental values of cyberspace have to be protected which includes making flexible policies for its security.

Still, these policies have to be following economic development. Many researchers compare different strategies, for example, if you compare the cybersecurity strategy of the United States of America and the European Union, and then later you compare these two with few more, you will notice that they all have a similar vision that addresses cybersecurity.

In the last few decades, there was an effort to transfer cybersecurity to be theoretical rather than practical discipline. The purpose was to make a science out of cybersecurity so it could provide a common ground for such amount of different cybersecurity topics. FAS or The Federation of American Scientists addressed this tendency in the following definition: "The challenge in defining science of cyber-security derives from the peculiar aspects of the field. The 'universe' of cyber-security is an artificially constructed environment that is only weakly tied to the physical universe." According to this, Cybersecurity is a very complex discipline and it requires an understanding of many other fields such as economics, computer science, clinical medicine, and other sciences that can be used for analogies for further research.

At the end of their report, the Federation concluded that "There is a science of cyber-security. Because it is a science with adversaries, it uses and will use, many different tools and methods. For the future, as far as can be discerned, there will be new attacks on old technologies and new technologies that need to be defended." According to FAS, there is no doubt that Cybersecurity is a science, it even has mature subfields. However, they consider that it lacks fundamental concepts and definitions that are accepted and trusted. Also, they believe that when everybody accepts the scientific foundation of cybersecurity, it will be much easier to establish harmonization and common policy designs. It will also be easier to apply the shared principle approach and of course, implementation will be less complex than before.

Digital infrastructure today is based on open standards. This infrastructure is essential for any kind of operation that concerns cyberspace. Active work is needed if the goal is to make improved international standards, even more since these standards have to include diverse settings. They need to have international bodies such as ITU, IEC, ISO). Then they need to include national bodies such as DIN, BSI or ANSI, and finally, these international standards have to meet consortia of industry standards as well.

It is said that technology with general-purpose along with general governance specifications mustn't lack security or privacy standards. Still, the amount of standards that can be seen as relevant is enormous due to the diversity on multiple levels. Mechanisms that are internationally recognized exist, and they are made to support the concept of open standards that we previously mentioned. An example of these standards is a World Trade Organization agreement. Contrarily, in cybersecurity, there are still perceptions that support local and national standards rather than international ones. According to this approach, local standards provide stronger security because their strategy is not as accessible as the international one.

On the other hand, many succeeded to disprove this attitude as misconception and continued working towards international standardization. Still, these standards might be inconvenient to the internet's global nature and they might limit the usage of the latest technologies. Few areas need to be developed when it comes to standardization. We will mention the most important ones:

The first one is to develop standards in cybersecurity strategies that can be used to address the current priorities. For example, that priority might be in the infrastructure area. The second area represents a lack of efficient processing, which means that the goal is to develop standardization flexibility so it can keep up with the dynamic changes in the technology environment. Many areas lack methods for harmonization, as we already mentioned. This is why one of the priorities of cybersecurity has to be a way of addressing the harmonization of policy standards on a global level. Lastly, there are no mechanisms that would allow regional requirements to be incorporated into the cybersecurity global nature without jeopardizing its standards and that nature itself.

This gaps that appear in standardization, mainly come from structural issues. We would point out that organizations all over the world, whether they are regional or international, work on developing standards that can be implemented as the most representative and efficient ones for cybersecurity. It is important to treat standardization of cybersecurity as a global rather than an isolated process, regardless of the context.

Chapter 5: Network Hacking

We have seen that the internet has become an inseparable part of our daily lives. Even though those online connections bring us advantages on multiple levels, there are risks that we can't avoid. Network hacking is one of these risks. However, before we talk about concrete hacking types and tools, we would like to explain some basic terms because they are a foundation of every potential network hacking attack, thus they are vulnerable.

Basic Terms to get Started

Firstly, you need to know what a computer network is. It is a group of computer systems that includes other hardware devices. All of these devices are linked together using communication channels. Communication channels facilitate the sharing of resources and full communication between all network users. Networks have their own categorization and it is commonly based on their characteristics. An example of the earliest networks is SAGE- the U.S. military's Semi-Automatic Ground Environment radar system. Another example is ARPANET from 1969 in which different universities were connected as a part of the ARPANET or Advanced Research Projects Agency Network project. Universities involved in the project were: the Stanford Research Institute, the University of Utah, the University of California at Los Angeles and the University of California at Santa Barbara. This project is important because it was the first version of what we know today as the Internet.

Networks have multiple applications, some of them are: to facilitate email communication, to enable video conferencing, to provide support for instant messaging, and so on. Networks are also used to connect more than one user to one hardware device such as a printer for example or to enable file sharing. Networks enable remote systems' operating programs and they are also the main responsible component for software sharing. Networks make it easier to access and forward information to other users. As we mentioned, there are several types of networks, however, here we are going to mention the commonly used ones:

- The first one is the LAN- Local Area Network that connects geographically close computers, like in the same building for example.

- The second one is WAN or the Wide Area Network. This network connects devices that use radio waves or telephone lines.

- The third network is the MAN or Metropolitan Area Network that uses data that are specifically designed for a certain city.

- The fourth network that we will mention is HAN or Home Are Network which connects all digital devices in a person's home.

- We will mention Intranet which is a network made for a certain company. Generally speaking, it is a network that you can access to find anything you need from the company or its property, and you can find anything related to it without going anywhere else. Intranet usually has private MANS and WLANs, and it also includes LAN networks.

- Extranet, on the other hand, is even more advanced because it includes an intranet from above, with an extended version. Extranet uses internal services and enables access to users who are not necessarily a part of the company, thus external.

- Also, there is the Internet or a network that allows external users to access all kinds of internal resources in different networks.

- There is a special type of network known as a virtual private network or VPN. This network is particular because it is secured. Its purpose is to provide a connection that goes across the public network such as the internet but it is still secured. Extranet networks usually use a VPN to establish a secure connection between a certain company and its recognized external users. VPN uses authentication that confirms the identities of both peers. This secured connection and network confidentiality are achieved through data encryption. This means that all data published and accessed within the VPN are private at all times.

Networking brings many advantages. Some of them are:

Firstly, file sharing, which means that through networking you can access, modify or copy all kinds of files that are not on your computer but you can access them through the network. It is a process as easy as having those files on your own computer. Another advantage is the ability to share resources. Good examples of this are fax machines or printers that we mentioned above, along with all kinds of storage devices, modems, webcams, and so forth.

The third advantage we will mention is program sharing. The important aspect of this ability is that you can use the network to share different programs and not only files. For example, if you have a word document, you can have a word document copy in the same program and just save it on the network. The document will run just like you open it from your own computer even though you are opening it from the network.

Another thing you should be familiar with is a network host. The more often used term is simply hosted, and it is a computer or some other device that is connected to the network. In fact, that device represents a kind of web server or terminal that is used to provide services for different types of clients.

A network protocol is also more commonly known as simply protocol. It represents a set of rules and conventions that two devices need to communicate. For instance, two computers won't be able to communicate using the network unless they both follow the protocols specified by the network. Some of the most known network protocol is an Internet protocol or IP address.

Internet protocol address or IP address is defined as a numerical label that every device should have. It is some kind of identification number, and each device participating in a network has to use IP addresses to communicate with some other device. There are two main functions of IP addresses: the first one is to identify a network and the second one is to locate it by using the address. IP addresses are always binary numbers even though they are frequently stored as text files so people can read it easier.

IP addresses can be categorized into public and private IP addresses. A private IP address is defined as "the one that is assigned to a computer on the Local Area Network (LAN)". On the other hand, a public IP address is seen as "the one that is assigned to a computer connected to the Internet". The most common way of computers connecting to the ISP network is by using a private IP address. Still, when you connect to the

ISP your computer is assigned a public IP address too which allows you to communicate with the internet. If you are not sure how to find your IP address it is quite straightforward, you just use Google and type "tell me my IP address". You should see it displayed in the search results immediately.

But if you want to view your private IP address the procedure is different. You need to open the prompt command window. You will find it by typing cmd into your "run" box. Then you need to enter the ipconfig/all command into the window and you will get a list of computer's details. IF you are interested only to see your IP address scroll down until you find "IPv4Address" or something similar, and that is your private IP address.

There are also different kinds of protocols. Some of them are:

HTTP or HyperText Transfer Protocol, and it represents a communication protocol. This protocol is used for information transfer on the Internet. HTTP responds to the client's request through a web browser and HTTP sends a response from its server.

Another protocol is FTP or File Transfer Protocol. This protocol provides a standard that is used for transferring files between two networks or two computers. The most common application of FTP is for upload/download operations that are operations that happen between a server and a workstation.

SMPT or Simple Main Transfer Protocol is a protocol that is used for sending e-mails from one server to another. This protocol is used by most email servers because it allows them to exchange communication between the servers.

Telnet is another network protocol that we will review. This protocol enables you to connect the remote hosts and the

Internet. Alternatively, you can connect a remote host to a local network. To do this, you need to have software that uses Telnet protocol and implements it to get the connection. Frequently, you will also need to have a username and a password to establish this connection. However, some hosts allow to connect as a guest, or they have a public network so you can connect easily. When you connect, you can use text commands to address the remote host.

WWW protocol, known as The World Wide Web or simply Web, is defined as a system of interlinked hypertext documents accessed via the Internet. If you open a web browser, you can use this protocol to view web pages that have different content such as text, images, videos, or other multimedia. Also, you can navigate between contents by hyperlinks. WWW protocol represents a collection of internet resources (like FTP, telnet, Usenet and so forth. Any kind of files such as hyperlinked text, audio, and video files, and remote sites can be accessed and searched by browsers if they use protocols that are based on HTTP or TCP/IP standards.

A program named Secure Shell or SSH was developed by SSH Communications Security Ltd. The purpose of this program is to use the network to log into another computer, so the user can execute commands in a remote machine. Also, SSH is used to move files from one device to another. The advantage of SHH was a strong and secure communication using authentication, even though the channels of that communication were rather insecure. In fact, we can say that Secure Shell is a substitute for login. Also, it can be a replacement for RCP, RDIST, and RSH.

This program protects used networks from hacking attacks like IP source routing for example. This means that if someone attacks the network, and succeeds to take over it, the only thing that an attacker can do with an SSH is to force it to disconnect. Otherwise, it is impossible to hijack the connection or view anything from the SHH's traffic once the encryptions start running. If you use Secure Shell instead of login, all data including password becomes encrypted, thus others can't crack it.

SSH port forwarding is a service from Secure Shell. It allows you to have a secure and encrypted connection even if you use non-encrypted services like e-mail for example. This service enables you to make a secure SSH (Secure Shell) session. Then it uses tunneled TCP connections to break through it. TCP works like this: it opens a connection, and then forwards a local port to a remote port that is placed over SHH. And then, the software of the SHH client (or email client if we take email as an example once again) is forwarded to the local port. The purpose of SHH port forwarding is to use passwords sent over non-encrypted channels and forward them as encrypted. This service is also known as SHH tunneling.

Domain Name System or DNS for shorts is a naming system that uses hierarchical structure from internet services and resources. DNS actually translates hostnames of every computer that is connected to the internet into an IP address. Also, DNS uses IP addresses to resolve hostnames just like the other way around. We can say that the Domain Name System is more like a large database. This database uses different devices and their IP addresses and name of multiple hosts or domains in general.

Domain Name System has its own structure that is shaped like a hierarchical tree. This tree starts with the top which is also called the "root". This "root" is labeled with a dot and it is followed by Top Level Domain or TLD. After TLD there is a name of the domain that is requested, and afterward, you can see many lower-level sub-domains. All of these sub-domains are separated from the dot that we mentioned above. TLD or Top Level Domains have two categories. The first one is called Generic TLD while the other one is called the Country Code TLD.

Here are some examples of Generic TLDs:

Commercial companies usually use ".com" TLD, nonprofit organizations mostly use ".org", institutions and schools mostly use ".edu" while various network infrastructures now use ".net". When it comes to Country Code TLDs, we will give some examples too: the United States use ".us", the United Kingdom uses ".uk", Russia, for instance, uses ".ru" domain, even small countries such as Montenegro have their own domains (for Montenegro ".me").

When it comes to authority, delegation, and zone of a certain domain, some rules have to be followed. For instance, the authority for every root domain and Generic TLDs is within ICANN or Internet Corporation for Assigned Numbers and Names. On the other hand, Country Code TLDs are not under ICCAN but under their own countries due to the administration benefits. As far as authorization goes, all levels in the hierarchy can control the next lower lever level in line.

DNS servers are running in all these levels and each level has an authority responsible for their own particular DNS. For instance, if a user sends an inquiry to get "www.thisisanexample.com", the root domain delegates this inquiry to its lower level, in this case ".com" generic TLD and leaves it there to be resolved. Then the DNS server from that lower level or ".com" sends a response with an IP address that contains the hostname, or www. Unlike authority, the zone represents only a part of a domain. For instance, if thisisanexample.com has all the information that a.thisisanexample.com has, maybe b.thisisanexample.com has the same data too. Still, the zone of thisisanexample.com has information related only to that domain and it further delegates the authorization to the sub-domains of servers in charge of execution. If the server doesn't have a sub-domain, then the zone and domain are basically the same things.

If you ever heard of a DNS query, you should know that it is basically something like asking a system what would be the IP address of a.thisisanexample.com. DNS can receive this kind of request for all sorts of domains even if it doesn't have any information about it. The DNS sends its response differently in that case. There are three kinds of DNS queries. The first one is known as a recursive query; the second one is the iterative query while the third one is known as an inverse query.

Before we start talking about hacking attacks and tools that you can use for hacking, we would like to mention one more important term that you have to be familiar with. We would like to introduce Proxy servers. A proxy server can be an application or a computer system. It behaves as an intermediate between the client's requests and servers that are providing resources to answer these requests. For example, the client requests a file or a webpage (a service) from a proxy server. The proxy server firstly evaluates this request. The purpose of the evaluation is to control the complexity of requests and simplify them if needed. Proxy servers were developed to support the structure of DNS. Nowadays, the majority of the proxy servers are in fact web proxies and they allow access and connections to WWW (World Wide Web) while guaranteeing anonymity.

There are various types of proxy servers. Still, we will mention some of the most common ones.

- The first proxy server type we will mention is called Anonymous Proxy. This proxy is used to make your information invisible. For example, if you use this proxy when requesting some files from a certain webpage, the webpage doesn't get your IP address. Instead, it gets the IP address of the proxy server you are using. This way, servers don't have any way of accessing your personal IP address and all of the communication that you have with the proxy server is encrypted. This proxy is especially significant for accessing information about things that need a lot of security.

- Another proxy type that we will view is called High Anonymity Proxy. This server goes even further, and it is not even identified as a server when you use it to request a service. It doesn't only conceal your own IP address; it doesn't even show its original IP address. This type of proxies use a header that is added to the proxy's IP address and it appears as the proxy server is a client instead of you.

- Transparent Proxy, on the other hand, is a server that receives your request, and then forwards it to the root server for resources without covering your IP. This kind of proxy server is mostly used in workplaces since IP addresses can be uncovered there. However, the advantage of this proxy is the fact that it can provide access to multiple computers' resources. Still, these proxies are usually not the first choice for many users.

- Lastly, Reverse Proxy is a server that is used to send requests from the internet or opened servers through private or isolated networks. This kind of proxy is usually used to prevent delicate data from being used in undesired situations and by unwanted clients on the internet. A reverse proxy can also be used to minimize the network traffic by using cash information instead of forwarding requests and waiting for an answer from servers with desired content.

Network Hacking and Hacking Tools

There are all sorts of risks when having a large amount of data on networks. Hacking attacks can be divided into active and passive attacks. We will view both of these types and then see some of the most commonly used network hacking tools.

When it comes to active attacks, we will mention masquerade attacks, session replay attacks, message modification attacks, denial of service attack and distributed denial of service attacks.

- Masquerade attack happens when a hacker uses your account (pretends to be you) and uses the system to take over information or privileges of the original user (or you in this case) without authorization. The most common way of performing this attack is stealing account passwords or IDs. The hacker uses gaps in the programs' security system and then it bypasses the mechanism of authentication to perform this action.

- Active attack named Session Replay is an attack in which a hacker uses the login information of the authorized uses and it steals the ID of the whole session. Hacker gets access and can perform any action like the original user.

- The third type of active attack that is quite common is named Message Modification and, as its name suggests, it is used to modify data for the targeted device by altering the packet header address.

- There are two additional attacks that we would like to point out. The first one is DoS or Denial of Service. If a hacker uses this kind of attack, you won't have access to a certain network anymore. The easiest way to achieve this is to overwhelm the targeted user with the amount of traffic it can't handle. The second attack is DDoS or Distributed Denial of Service.

  As its name suggests, it uses many systems that are previously compromised and then it attacks just one target. This type of attack is also known as the zombie army.

Unlike active attacks, passive attacks use networks to monitor them, and more often to scan them to find vulnerabilities of a certain system. The purpose of passive attacks is nothing more but collecting information, and it is difficult to spot because there are no visible data changes. There are two kinds of passive attacks, the first one is active reconnaissance, and the second one is called passive reconnaissance.

The first one uses port scans which means that the hacker must engage with the system it targets, while the second type uses monitoring systems without any interaction. One of the most commonly used methods of passive attacks is known as Wardriving. This method targets WI FI networks that are weak. It scans them if the attacker is nearby. Typically, the WI FI is scanned by using a portable antenna. This method can be harmless, like stealing an internet connection, but on the other hand, it can be an activity to test and map Analyzing networks and software.

The ability to change network information such as IP addresses, for example, is one of the most useful skills that you have to learn. It allows you to access all kinds of networks, and you will appear to administrators and other users as a device that they can trust. Let's say that there is a DoS attack if you know how to handle spoofing of your IP address you will be able to lead those who inspect the source of attack that it came from somewhere else. In Kali Linux and Linux in general, if you know the right command it is not that difficult. In this case, you can use '' the ifconfig" command, or you can use '' ifconfigfollowed" to simply change your IP address completely. We will give a concrete example of the code that can be used, and let's say that the new IP address we want to assign to our device is 191.268.191.225 and that the interface is ''eth0''. The code would be as follows:

kali >ifconfigeth0191.268.191.225 kali >

If you do this right, Kali will do the rest, it will return the command which is a good thing, because when you check your IP address next time using the ''ifconfig'' command you should be able to see your new IP address, thus the one you assigned to your device.

DNS or Domain Name System is often a target of hackers. DNS, in particular, is seen as one of the most critical components when it comes to the internet. The purpose of DNS indeed is to make IP addresses out of domains; however, hackers use it to get the information they need about the network or device they observe as a target.

There are few ways to inspect DNS, but the most commonly used one is to use services from websites such as www.hackersarise.com and simply translate the desired domain name into the IP address so your system immediately knows how to obtain what it needs. If there were no DNS's each of us would have to memorize a large number of IP addresses for each website that we want to visit- without exceptions. This is where the " dig" command comes in, and it is a command that helps you get the information about the domain you are interested in using DNS. If you store the information you gathered using DNS properly, you can be in a real advantage of the targeted network environment. You can even obtain sub-domains and their IP addresses if needed.

For all these advantages, it is necessary to know at least fundamental networking skills in Linux. You should be able to manage networks, connect to them and analyze them before you start doing more advanced things.

Another basic task that a person interested in Kali Linux should know how to perform is how to add software or how to remove it. Installing software that you didn't get by default is a very frequent thing, and it is not uncommon that you have software that you get but you don't need it. Also, you may have software that won't run unless you add the second software that will run it. An additional scenario is downloading software packages (file groups) that you need to successfully execute tasks. These packages are usually different libraries that contain files essential to various tasks. Installing a package means that you will get a large number of files together and that you will get a script to help you load the software successfully.

To download a software package that you need, the first step is to see if it's located in your own repository, rather than looking for it online. A repository is a place in your operating system that contains all the information needed for a fully functional system. To search for the packages inside the local repository you can use the "apt" tool, which has a function to search. Once you execute this command, you will immediately know if the package you were looking for is available or not.

If you establish that the package is available in the local repository, the next thing you do is you use "apt-get" to download the software and install its peace directly to the operating system that you are using at the moment. The "apt-get" command should be always used with a keyword, in this case "install and" and you add the name of the software package you need to install.

On the other hand, if you want to remove software, you will use the same " apt-get" command but the difference will be adding the "remove option" along with the name of the software package you want to delete. All these operations are visible in real-time, and you will always receive a question if you wish to continue your action or not. There are two commands you can use for uninstalling software: command "yto" is used to completely uninstall it, but if you use "snort" it will save it in case you want to use it again.. Keep in mind that commands for removal don't delete configuration files from the operational system, so it is possible to reinstall the package you removed before without having to download the same configuration again. If you, however, want to completely remove the package and its configuration, there is a "purge" option that will allow you to execute that.

Like most of the software components, repositories will also have updates. These updates will mostly come once the new version of the existing software comes out. Still, in most cases, you won't get these updates automatically, which means that you will have to order them and then apply them to your operating system by yourself. Note that updating and upgrading is not the same thing! Updates stand for a list of packages that you can download from the repository that you are using. On the other hand, the upgrade represents the last version of that same repository. To update the system, you can use the "apt-get" command just like before, the only difference is that now you use the keyword update with it. After this command is executed, you will get the list of the available updates, if there are any.

Another thing that you should be aware of is that sometimes software that you need won't be available on a repository that you have. This will likely happen if the software is a new release. So you have to find an alternative to obtain it. The frequently used website that you might find useful in these situations is https://www.github.com. This site is actually a place where developers connect and they have the possibility of sharing software with other people. Here you can find a lot of useful things and get feedback on things you are interested in from the people of the same interests. The website is simple to use, and you can just go to "search" and type the software that you are interested in. If there is a result that matches your search, you will see a full repository and get the package that you need by using the "gitclone" command and URL of the repository to put it into your system.

Permissions, Processes, And User Environment Variables

Normally, different users have different levels of access when it comes to the operating system's directories and files. Kali Linux has its methods for securing access just like all other operational systems. Its security system enables the administrator otherwise known as the root user to secure its files from any person that wants to tamper with data. This security is achieved by granting user permissions to selected people.

These permissions concern writing, reading or executing different files for each directory separately. There is even an option of specifying the owner of files for all users or just for a group of users. Every operating system that has multiple users has different ways of limiting access to others whether they are groups or individuals, otherwise, there would be chaos. Different levels of permissions refer to different kinds of permissions, and we will discuss some of them in the following paragraphs. The ability to understand how permissions work will level you up in exploiting a certain system.

In Kali Linux, just like in Linux in general, the main administrator can do anything that he or she wants with the system and inside the system. All other users have more or less limited access, depending on their role and permissions obtained from the administrator. But in most cases, only the root user has that amount of authority in the entire operating system and no other users are equal to him when it comes to the matter of access.

Contrarily, all other users are mostly gathered into groups with different kinds of permissions. Their groups are based on similarities in their function, or generally speaking, they are most frequently divided into groups such as sales, engineering, finance, marketing, and so forth. Still, since we talk about jobs that include the IT sector, it is more likely that these groups are developers, database experts, administrators of the networks, etc. The group concept is simple, you take people that have similar roles and interests and you give them permission relevant for their work. This way every member of the group inherits the same permission that is necessary to complete their daily tasks. This way of work is essential for security in every operating system and it makes it easier to detect if there are some inconsistencies. When you add a new user to the system, you must add him or her to one of the groups, otherwise, it won't get any access to the system.

To grant permission means that you need to allocate each file and each directory and make a different level of access for different groups or individuals that will use it. There are three levels of permissions in a system:

- Permission to read (r). This permission allows you to view files and nothing else.

- Permission to write (w). This permission enables you to edit files other than view it.

- Finally, there is a permission to execute (x). With this permission, you can execute a certain file, but that doesn't mean that you can do either of the actions mentioned above.

This way, the administrator makes sure that everyone gets only those permits that are necessary for completing tasks. So it means that in most cases the person who creates the file is viewed as the owner of that file while the group in which the user belongs has group ownership over it

You can give ownership of a file to another user, that way you grant him or her a permission to control the file and who else has access to it. To do that you can use "chown" command which simply means –change the owner. The command can be like this for example:

kali >chown❶mary❷/tmp/marysfil

As you can see, in this case, we changed the ownership along with the name and location of the file. Now Mary (❶) has the ownership of the file we named marysfile (❷).

The change mode command is used to change the type and level of permission. Note that the only person that can use this command is the administrator of the operating system. There are two methods of executing ''chmod'' that we will view. The first one is numeric and the second one is symbolic.

The first method, or the numeric one, is actually the method that uses decimal notation to change permissions. It refers to a shortcut that can be created by using just one number that represents certain permission. Operating systems use binary representation to represent almost everything, and this is no exception. In this case, number 1 represents ''on'' while 0 represents ''off'' switch for a permit. If you remember there are three types of permissions if we incorporate that with binary switches, three number ones (111) will mean that the user has the permission to view, edit and execute a file. When you have this kind of binary set there is an option of representing it as a single digit. For this, you will use an octal digit that consists of three binary digits.

Even though the previous method is far more popular than the one we are about to mention, the symbolic method is considered to be more intuitive. Note that there are no particular differences in the quality of performance between both of these methods; the only thing that makes a distinction between them is your personal preference. The symbolic method is also known as the UGO syntax which is very simple, and the meaning of UGO is actually user-group-others.

If you want to change the permission using this method you can enter the change mode command and add ''u if you want to change permission for user, "g" if you want to change permission for group, and "o" if you want to change the permission for others. Additionally, you have to follow these two parts with one of the three operators. You can either add "-" to remove permission, "+" to add permission and "=" if you want to set the permission. When you add the operator you have to include the permission type and the name of the file that the permission refers to.

There is an even more secure way of setting permissions, and it is known as giving permissions with masks. An operating system such as Linux has base permissions that are automatically assigned for files and directories. For example, files are assigned with 666 permission while directories have 777 one. Of course, there is a way of changing default permissions for both of them, and you can do it by using the unmask method. This method is also known as "umask" and it stands for permission that has to be removed from the automatic base permissions allocated on a certain directory or file. This way, those files and directories have more security.

The unmask method uses a decimal number of three digits that are correspondent with the three digits of permissions that we have already mentioned several times. However, "umask" is subtract off the number of permissions that gives a new status of the user. Generally speaking, this means that when you create a new directory (or file, it doesn't matter), you don't have a classic default permission value. Instead, you have a default value minus "unmask" value as the final status of that directory

Now, all types of permissions that we mentioned above are actually permissions for general purposes. Alternatively, there are three special kinds of permissions, and they are considered to be more complicated than the one that refers to viewing editing or executing files. Special permits, on the other hand, refer to SUID (set user ID), SGID (set group ID), and the last one is known as sticky bit

By now, it is clear that it is impossible to work with a file or a directory if you don't have permission to access it. Although in general, those who have r or w permissions can't execute for example, there are some exceptions. Some files may need administrator's approval regardless of the type of permission they have (even if they have one to execute).

For instance, if you want to change your password, you need to access the file type that contains passwords in the operational system. This file needs the root user's (administrator's) approval to execute this kind of action even though the user has the permission to change its own password. Still, in these types of situations, you can give a temporary privilege that will allow users who are not administrators to execute files without additional approvals.

You can do that by setting a SUID in the program. You add "SUIDbit" command that stands for special permission that doesn't extend to any other file and it doesn't require any additional execution approvals. If you want to set this you just add four before the number of the regular permission attached to that file.

The sticky bit is the third kind of special permission that we mentioned. It is set to allow someone to rename or delete files within the directory that permit refers to. Still, this permit is actually from before, only before it was known as UNIX which is ignored by most of the modern operating systems.

User Environment Variables

Understanding the environment variables is one of the crucial aspects that you have to understand if you want to get the most of any operating system. Additionally, you have to be able to manage them and if necessary adapt them to have at least optimal performance at all times. This also means that the system has to be convenient and stealth. In Linux, for example, most of the newcomers have big issues with mastering the management processes of the environment for users and variables that influence that environment. We can say that there are two main types of user variables: environmental and shell

When it comes to the first type of environmental variables, we can define them as variables that your system uses to control the way it feels like to the user. They define the way that the system will look and act like for the user too. Environment variables can be inherited from "child" processes or shells that we will mention next. So, we just mentioned shells, they are important to us to understand another type of variable known as shell variables. These variables are only valid if they are set in the particular shell they are connected to. Unfortunately, the scope of this book doesn't cover deeper differences between environmental and shell variables, it just sets them as very useful skills that you should be aware of

A shorter definition of variables can be viewing them as pairs that have key value in the operating system. So, we can say that all pairs are presented as key=value and if there are more values in a row, we can write them down as KEY=value1:value2:value3:value4 and so on. Taking Linux or Kali Linux into consideration, we can say that the value spaces are represented as quotation marks and that, specifically in

Kali, the user environment can be represented as a sum of bash shells.

Also, keep in mind that all users have their own set of environment variables that are assigned to them by default, and the administrator is no exception. These assigned variables establish the look and the actions of the system for each user individually. If you want to customize the system according to your own preferences you should change the values of your variables.

It is also important to know that there is a way of viewing all environment variables at once. You can get insight into local variables, shell variables, and their functions along with their command aliases. To achieve this you can use the "set" command which will show you a list that is unique for your system at the moment. With this command, you can access variables separately too, viewing them one by one, line by line.

Inspecting Wireless Networks

We will view two types of wireless network inspection, the one using the "IFCONFIG" tool, and the one using " IWCONFIG".

First, the "ifconfig" command is the command we have already mentioned and it represents one of the most commonly used tools for inspecting interfaces of active networks whether they are wireless or not. If you execute this command you will get the query of your connections to active networks. This command can provide you information that can be useful when examining active networks on the system. Therefore, it is not surprising that the first output that you get is the name of the network.

When examining networks, interface usually appears as "eth0" which stands for Ethernet (in Linux and Kali Linux that we use as examples ,0 is used more than number 1 for this output). This means that you have detected a wired network, and if there are more, you will just have more "eth" with numbers that increase respectively (eth1, eth2, eth3, etc.). The next thing that you can see is the IP address, that we have also mentioned in the sections above. After it, network examination shows you broadcast address that actually represents the location of all information that is sent to different IP addresses. In the end, you can see "the mask" of the network. This mask is actually a pointer that shows you if the local network and IP address are connected.

There is a section that shows another kind of network connections, it is a special software address that is used to connect a network to its own system, however, services that are not directly on your system will not be able to use that network. Lastly, there is a wlan0 type of connection that appears when you have a wireless interface, or when you have a wireless adapter. You are also able to get the MAC address of the adapter if needed which allows you to use and change settings on your local area network which is one of the fundamental hacking skills.

Now, another type of wireless network inspection is connected directly to the wireless adapter, and you can do it by using the "iwconfig" command. This tool helps you collect the most important information that you can later use for hacking or penetration testing. The kinds of basic information that you will get using this inspection are MAC and IP addresses of the targeted adapter, the mode of that adapter, and other useful info that you can later apply using "aircracking". "Aircracking" is a tool for hacking that gives you outputs for wlan0 wireless extensions. That is the expected and necessary result. With this tool, you can become aware of wlan0 capabilities that you weren't aware of before. There are standards that devices are capable of doing and a way of communication that they can do. As you might suggest, most wireless adapters today have these standards and extensions that include different kinds of modes. With the inspection of the above-mentioned type, we can easily determine the mode of the wireless adapter, crack its password, see if it has an access point and the strength of its signal.

Chapter 6: Tying it all Together

In previous chapters, we talked about scripting as a basis of every computer operation and its significance. Then we discussed cybersecurity as one of the most important aspects of data protection. Lastly, we viewed basic hacking definition and what are some common terms that you need to know to fully understand the importance of networks that already became a part of our daily lives. All of these things are connected and represent a foundation for one another.

For example, without the evolution of scripting, there wouldn't be any networks. Without networks, there wouldn't be any hackers, and without hackers that wouldn't be any need for cybersecurity strategies. Still, the only way to talk about tying these three areas together is to talk about how they correlate with each other. And since scripting is a constant behind both, hacking and cybersecurity, we will return to explaining these correlations using mainly these two areas.

You could conclude that cybersecurity is a growing challenge. Also, it is constant in many aspects. And regardless of developing more and more secure software products and upgrading approaches, hackers follow and become better equipped and more and more skillful. Not only that, even their markets are growing, and reachable values are both important and expensive. On the other hand, these highly skilled attacks and their frequency forced many organizations to look for better protection of their properties, especially when it comes to data protection. Since the complexity of these intermingled topics is very complex, there is still so much to do before something changes radically.

Many people consider cybersecurity to be a secret world. The reason for this is quite understandable, it is a duty of organizations in charge of cybersecurity to protect as much information as possible from disclosure. Concealing data is one of the strategies that can prevent hacking attacks. Of course, it is impossible to conceal everything, but at least some practices that are unreachable to the public can make a big difference. Furthermore, one of the reasons why cybersecurity isn't getting ahead of the network hacking attacks is, as some researchers say, its short-sighted analysis.

These analyses mainly focus on the classification of malware that can happen to networks instead of focusing on the effects of hacking activities and establish whether these effects are long term or short term. Those interesting in hacking and attacking networks with malicious intents are not bothered by statistics; they are more concerned about subverting computers.

But subverting software that is diligently written often means that there is a path to elude the attention of those who keep the system safe, thus compromise the defended network. However, it is difficult to do this because holes in defense are not opened for long so hacking attack frequently depends on the ability to find a defense hole that is not watched tightly.

That is one of the few ways to make a surprise attack since hacking attempts are no longer a surprise per se. Besides, that was one of the main reasons why we have mentioned the importance of understanding the cyberspace and its evolution. In the Giles research published in 2014, it was estimated that organizations and governments across the world spend around 70 billion dollars per year on cybersecurity alone. It was also estimated that that amount will grow at least 10%

each year and that it is practically impossible to decrease this amount.

On the contrary, it would be wrong to say that organizations are not completely satisfied with the state of cybersecurity nowadays. We can say that the general attitude is, that the strategies developed by now, should give the upper hand against hacking attacks for at least a few years. One can argue about the relations between the expenditures and success rates and if that relationship is effective enough.

There are, in fact, approaches that claim how hackers aren't far behind defense systems at all. The purpose of tying together scripting, cyberspace, and hacking is to try to understand better the basic forces that are driving cybersecurity. Also, the purpose is to provide us with maximum benefits and data protection. Many additional aspects influence this tie. Some of them are industry, (in this case cybersecurity can be viewed as a separate industry), and the products that offer, software development, and so forth. Determining the "friend and a foe" border is rather difficult, especially when it comes to software.

The same product can be both depending on the intentions of its user. That is why it is important to comprehend how scripting, hacking, and cybersecurity interact. You will also learn how their purposes intermingle constantly in this context. Cost-effective solutions are one of the many struggles that are yet to be discussed. There is a lot of money involved, regardless of the area of your observation. It can be cybersecurity or hacking and its market.

The main goal of every cybersecurity strategy is to achieve the best possible results while minimizing costs. The reason why cybersecurity involves a lot of money is that the expenditures are expensive. Also, if a cyberattack happens, enormous amounts of money are needed to recover from the attack. For example, these costs include the down-time of the hacked network, recovery costs (especially if there where information about technological discoveries, prototypes, and so on), and costs regarding reputation loss. It is difficult to measure the consequences of the attack, thus it is not possible to predict how many resources are needed in case someone successfully hacks the network. It is extremely difficult to predict negative costs (if, for example, it happens that the hacking attack was prevented). It is also almost impossible to measure the impact of a cyberattack on the organization not only because it lost valuable information, but also the reputation and trust of its users.

On the other hand, hackers are not uninterested in money, they also have their costs and benefits to calculate, and they are well aware of the market and its signals. Hackers always calculate the amount of work they have to do and the reward that they will get. For example, they will always measure how much effort they need to put into penetrating a network, how dangerous it is, and what will they gain for it. In general, their costs are lower than those from the cybersecurity side, but their gains can be even higher.

Also, the difficulty of the system's defense is measured by the amount of effort that hacker needs to invest to crack it. Some systems are so difficult to crack, that many hackers don't want to do it because they find it unprofitable. Furthermore, networks that have strong defense systems require a skillful person to break through them. So, the harder the defense system, the fewer hackers can crack it. Still, every organization that wants to be secure has to develop almost impenetrable systems, otherwise, they are never completely secure.

Even though there are many different cyberattacks, there are tendencies that imply how some of these attacks have constant advanced threats and they usually come in two stages. The first one is achieved by penetrating the targeted system (computer). The second stage refers to the leverage that hackers use once they penetrate the network. Then, they can move through the system and compromise whatever part of the network they want.

Being able to prevent penetration of the system depends on several factors. Still, one of the most important ones is software and the system that the client uses. Keep in mind that this includes web browsers, add-ons and so on and that they should possess certain qualities. Having administrated software for hacking preventions should be one of the overall goals. There should always be a service that provides security for the entire system.

Hackers have their own adversaries, so it often happens that every measure that is given at the cybersecurity strategy already has a countermeasure designed by hackers. The extent of these countermeasures that negate defense efforts can be different in their implementation and efficiency. We will mention two countermeasures that we find most interesting. The first one concentrates on tools that are hackers develop, and the ability of those tools to work below the visibility of the tools implemented by cybersecurity organizations. In contrast, it can be interesting to observe how organizations react to such tools and what investments they make to recover from their defense failure.

The second countermeasure refers to the efforts that hackers put into finding software flaws. There is a lot of techniques used by organizations to make their software as flawless as possible in terms of their security. Still, hackers can countermeasure it with their ability to find those rare vulnerabilities. Sometimes these hackers are white hats and they are actually testing the system, but the point is, there is still a possibility to beat the system's defense.

There are many specific characteristics for these events in terms of business type, company size, type of employees, amount of many on disposal, network types and so on. We will discuss some of these specific situations. First of all, security postures are connected to the type and size of the company, as we already mentioned, which means that most frequently small businesses don't have solutions that are as good as solutions to big companies.

Also, the important aspect is intellectual property, and its importance depends on the particular mission of the firm. Cybersecurity is very expensive and still has to be improved which means that it is hard to sell it, even more, if you want to sell it to the chief executives of the big companies. Since there is no way to know how much money is exactly spent on cybersecurity, and even if that amount was enough, the company is usually divided on those who think it is, and those who think that it is not enough.

It can be useful to know about the existence of air-gapping. If you use air-gapping it means that you electronically isolate all networks from the internet. Air-gapping is often compared with tunneling that we also mentioned in previous chapters, which means that networks tunnel through the internet without making any interactions with it. It is interesting that in some companies, asking to connect personal devices to business networks can cause a lot of dilemmas, especially if there is a doubt of a potential cyber-attack.

Many companies consider that hackers have the upper hand when it comes to cyberspace and that they will have it for a long time. It is not unusual to have customers that want powerful solutions for security without even knowing what kind of tools exist and even if it is well known that no magic can protect a device completely. At least it wasn't invented yet. Many organizations give priority to human-centric options when investing more in cybersecurity. Frequently, companies want to know the methods that certain hackers use, or what kind of motives hackers can have to attack. However, there is no consensus on the usage of that kind of information.

So-called cyber insurance at the moment is described by many companies as "having more hassles than benefits". Additionally, many support the approach of cybersecurity being useful only in specific situations and having little to offer in return for a great deal of money that has to be invested in it. On the other hand, some approaches claim how active defense has multiple benefits. However, they also argue that it evokes an insufficient amount of enthusiasm, and that lack of many definitions impacts its growth.

There are other things that companies find difficult to accept when it comes to cybersecurity. Some of them are incentives and non-existence of their vision. Others are linked with trust and the fact that sharing information at this point tends to be done just within the people that are trusted by the company. Many companies have doubts about cloud services because many people are just followers without the desire to buy, and their point of view is that being exposed to privacy breaches is one of the reasons why customers are cautious.

It is not uncommon that organizations to assign a lower priority to cybersecurity than they should, which is why the chance of a successful network attack increases. Some of the hacking impacts that might surprise you are, for example, reputation influences. Many organizations and business companies consider that being under a cyberattack affects reputation severely, and that alone costs them more than the monetary loss they had to give on obtaining defenses in the first place.

The point is that, in these situations, if the client knows that data is at risk it means that the company will have more loses than having intellectual property affected during the attack. Generally speaking, it is still not fully understand how to measure loss and how to estimate the process of recovery.

The ability of hackers to find countermeasures or tools to undermine cybersecurity measures are escalating all the time. This means that the growth of cybersecurity means that the hackers evolve too. For example, if we use firewall filtering, the basic one, and grain signature and examinations of because there was an intrusion alarm, we can prevent an attack and activate deep packet inspection.

In time, organizations and business companies became aware that they can reduce potential hacking attacks and their impact by using DLP or data loss prevention programs. Additionally, they learned that there are multiple uses of private networks that are virtual (VPNs) that we discussed in some of the previous chapters. Still, hackers have solutions for this too, they use obfuscation, stealth, and other malware to penetrate the system. Cybersecurity started focusing on observing the behavior of the network rather than its signatures to determine if there is an attack. It is not rare that hackers and cybersecurity specialists use the same tools, but for different purposes. It became very difficult to establish the quality of work coming from cybersecurity specialists because every measure they come up with is always breached by hackers' countermeasures.

It is said that the only way for cybersecurity specialists to get the upper hand is to make networks and software static. Since that is practically impossible, we can conclude that the upper hand can be achieved but it doesn't last long. Innovation is the main characteristic of technology, and since the innovation process is alive, there is no way to make it stop. In comparison, if networks were to become more complicated, security might have the advantage of progressing faster.

A software system named "Walled garden" is a software in which the provider has control over overall communication, transactions, and content. And it is proved that this software, for example, is harder to hack than software systems that are opened. However, hacking trends didn't vent exactly in that direction. In the last 20 years, there was a much larger reliance on network open systems along with the software ones. The key element of having successful cybersecurity is to develop a good system software.

Many companies invest much more money in increasing their cybersecurity just because their initial software is weak and not secure enough. Having good software with a solid defense system from its foundation represents a good head start in preventing hacking attacks and making it hard for hackers to gain access to the targeted network. This particular type of prevention is known as the external hardness of a business company or organization. Still, if the hacker penetrates through this initial defense, additional ones are needed if the company wants to prevent hackers from obtaining information that can be harmful to them (known as the internal hardness of business company or organization).

We can say that hackers can find the weaknesses or vulnerabilities of software by using its design, or even simpler, through the implementation of faults or coding. Subsets hacker gets from these examinations are exploitable. This means that a hacker can do all sorts of unintended actions by using remote code execution. This remote code execution refers to complete control given to the certain actor who can do whatever wants in the targeted system.

Usually, software weak spots are fixed before the software is even released. On the other hand, it can happen that the customer realizes that there are vulnerabilities after purchasing software and then the company fixes it. However, there are times where some customers discover some software weaknesses and don't report it to the company. There are few markets where that customer can sell this kind of information: if the information is given to the vendor it means that it is on the white market, If the information is sold to the government it means that it is on the gray market. Lastly, if this kind of information is sold to hackers or cybercriminals, it means that it is on the black markets.

Finding software weakness is not a trivial matter which means that it is very valuable. On the other hand, fixing these vulnerabilities often represents an even bigger issue for the company. Even if that's not the biggest problem, there are malware that appears and picks up weaknesses of the software even after patches for fixing them were released. Still, trends in software designs point outs that there is a significant improvement when it comes to several weaknesses.

As you know, a lower amount of vulnerabilities means a lower risk of hacking attacks. But the question that still needs to be answered is what mechanisms can be used to improve defense once the hacker enters the network rather than upgrading prevention only. This means that there are still not enough solutions for minimizing damage in case an attack happens and that everyone is mostly focused on preventing the damage.

Three internet browsers are most frequently used on the whole internet. These browsers are Google Chrome, Internet Explorer and Mozilla Firefox. All three browsers evolve around corrupted web pages that can propagate their created faults only within the browser and not on the operating system of the computer used to connect to it. Additionally, there are many improvements that browsers themselves are experiencing.

The reason for this is mostly because there are constant patches that help them become more automated than in the previous version. Also, with these improvements, they need even more sophisticated campaigns to become infected. We would add that there is a large amount of complex relationship with IoT or the internet of things also discussed in the previous chapters. These relationships bare privileges that might be required to some other similar organization which improves integration.

Efforts of cybersecurity strategies in this context should be based on the premise that hackers already penetrated the network and that the defense goal is to manage system security more intensively not on a network level but rather on the systematic one. Some researches see this as a better strategy than just focusing all resources on preventing hacking attacks. There were some cybersecurity models developed over the years, and some of them were designed to demonstrate how to lower costs coming from the cyberspace insecurities. Just to clarify, these costs contain several types of costs. The final sum is the result of adding direct and indirect costs. These costs can be from cyberattack losses for example, or direct costs that an organization has from training users, they can be connected with different restrictions, thus indirect costs, and so on.

We would point out that the odds of having every device (whether it is a computer or a smartphone) successfully defend against the hacking attacks can be predicted only by calculating the number of devices and the quality of software that each device uses. This way it is possible to determine the level of external hardness of the company at the beginning. The company can upgrade its external hardness by training harder. It can prevent users from making changes on their own for example.

On the other hand, the internal hardness of the company can be increased to a level where it can buy tools for cybersecurity. Besides, external hardness can be increased using one more way, it can reduce the number of supported connected devices. This is achieved by using restrictions, thus limiting the content that users can put on the network. It is possible to lower the cyberattack costs if the company finds a way to isolate the part of the network that has the most valuable hacking information. This means that data that can be costly if compromised should not be a part of the network like all other data. Data security is, as you could see, one of the most important things nowadays. As the opposite of this, hacking skills are admirable in keeping up with cybersecurity development. Still, some priorities need to be established.

It is important to know what type of data you want to protect and how badly you want to protect it. This means that you should also consider what is worth protecting in the first place. From a company's perspective, the first priority is usually the company's reputation, and the second one is machines and applications that are connected to the network. One of the problem compounds in this part Is IoT because it includes a wide choice of devices that can be connected to the network.

It is also important to know in what direction you should turn to if you want to protect your personal data or in this case the company data. The main thing that needs to be decided here is how much defense is needed in internal workings and how much remains for the perimeter. It is not uncommon for hackers to be persistent and to create constant network presence. This means that if you open an attachment that was malware it sends you to the malicious site. If this happens, your system is already penetrated and it looks to weaken the code. This scripting enables the hacker to send the command that will certainly be executed in this kind of situation. If the penetrated code is weak, hackers won't have any additional issues. However, if the code is more difficult to override, the hacker will need more time. This doesn't mean that better codes can't be infected and that you won't need to use many different tools to resolve the problem.

Once you set all cybersecurity defenses you might think that the best solution is to wait to see how well they perform if some attack happens. However, you must realize that the best way to deal with hackers is to know what are you dealing with from the start. The best way is to see how their countermeasures work against the defenses you've set. It is a common practice that companies hire ethical hackers that would test their systems. Ethical hackers are hackers just like all others, but there is one big difference- they work with authorization. The most effective way of preparing yourself for a potential cyberattack is making sure that actual hacker can't crack your network, or at least to determine how difficult it would be to do so and is there any room for improvement.

Tying up scripting with cybersecurity and network hacking might seem like a paradox. Still, we can't deny that software is improving, cybersecurity strategies gain in complexity and hackers evolve making it difficult for all organizations to slow down with policy-making progress. There was an interesting observation that cybersecurity experts are actually hackers that could infiltrate any network but they didn't know how to take advantage of that knowledge or skills. Finally, it is undeniable that both, cybersecurity and hacking are profitable areas, therefore very attractive. Keep in mind that IoT enables even more paths that hackers can use for their activities. The challenges of today's data protection keep both sides busy, and there is no clear prediction when one of these sides will have a clear advantage over the other.

Conclusion

You've come to the finish line! Hopefully you've enjoyed what you've learned so far. Now, don't get too far ahead of yourself, you aren't quite a fully-fledged hacker yet, but you're well on your way. I hope that this book has managed to provide you with the knowledge and skills that you'll find necessary on your road to learning how to become a real cybersecurity expert, or who knows, maybe even a hacktivist.

It's worth keeping in mind that your job has barely begun, if at this point, you feel like you might not like hacking, then it's probably best to rethink it as your career choice. You do not want to be trapped in a career you don't really love, and if hacking is that for you, then you won't succeed even if you tried.

Naturally, due to the high learning curve for hackers, there's a variety of jobs that are offered to them. This means that, as a hacker, you should expect to land jobs even outside of your area of expertise. Let's say you're an expert white hat hacker that has multiple Google challenges under their belt. Well, landing a mid-level programming gig after all that can't really be a challenge. This means you have a lot of flexibility in your career. If at any point you decide hacking isn't for you, you can simply get employed as a programmer, IT expert, sysadmin and others.

You'll find that experience as a cybersecurity expert is very desirable in a wide variety of fields. Even if you went to apply as say, an accountant, your recruitment manager would think about how your background ensures your computer expertise. Furthermore, the company would feel more comfortable with their private numbers in your hands. Now, if you do choose to pursue a career in cybersecurity, then there are two ways to do it. Freelance and with an employer.

Working with an employer is like any other job really. You go to interviews, apply for jobs at companies, end up getting promoted, rinse and repeat. It's the traditional formula, however, even like this you should expect to be earning well in the six-figure range in a few years.

A good part of your job as a cybersecurity expert is that you can do it remotely. This allows you to travel for as long and as much as you want, all while working off of the surface of your laptop. This is why so many cybersecurity experts have adopted this "digital nomad" lifestyle.

Freelancing on the other hand, is a whole different beast. It's basically like holding your own little business. You'll be your own boss, you'll decide your own hours and manage your own income. On the other hand, this does come with some downsides. For example, you will actually need to advertise yourself and seek out clients manually. Furthermore, no client is ever stable, so you'll need to keep a balance of multiple clients at all times.

This can be rather difficult, especially when just starting out. If you choose the freelance route, unless you have some crazy skills, there are two main ways to find work:

The first is by finding traditional employment first. This gives you experience after which it can be a lot easier to go freelance. Plus, if you like employment you might just stay like that. This will help you get into the market, and it's possible that once you get skilled enough, the same company that employed you as a worker will employ you as a freelancer later down the line, only for a much better sum of money.

The other route is starting out with an aggregate like UpWork. Personally I'd advise against this. They offer freelance jobs that you apply to, and then they take a solid cut. The reason I don't like these sites is not just the large cut though, it's also that as a beginner, you'll have to do jobs that are very underpaid.

In the book following this one, we'll be delving deeper into most subjects already covered by this one. We'll dive deeper into Kali Linux (our distro of choice) and teach you how to use it. We'll also go over Bash scripting in much more depth than we did here. You'll find that the text-filled sections of this book are slowly going away, and making way for cold, hard code.

Made in the USA
Coppell, TX
26 July 2020

31662072R00079